WITH
REVERENCE
AND AWE

WITH
REVERENCE
AND AWE

Returning to the Basics of
Reformed Worship

D. G. HART and
JOHN R. MUETHER

P U B L I S H I N G
P.O. BOX 817 • PHILLIPSBURG • NEW JERSEY 08865-0817

Unless otherwise indicated, Scripture quotations are from the NEW AMERICAN STANDARD BIBLE®. ©Copyright The Lockman Foundation 1960, 1962, 1963, 1968, 1971, 1972 1973, 1975, 1977, 1995. Used by permission.

Scripture quotations from the American Standard Version (ASV) ©copyright Thomas Nelson & Sons 1901, International Council of Religious Education 1929. Scripture quotations from the Revised Standard Version (RSV) ©copyright Division of Christian Education of the National Council of Churches of Christ in the United States of America 1946, 1952, 1971.

Italics within Scripture quotations indicate emphasis added.

Page design and typesetting by Lakeside Design Plus

Printed in the United States of America

Library of Congress Cataloging-in-Publication Data

Hart, D. G. (Darryl G.)
　　With reverence and awe : returning to the basics of reformed worship / D. G. Hart and John R. Muether.
　　　　p.　cm.
　　Includes bibliographical references and index.
　　ISBN 0-87552-179-7 (pbk.)
　　1. Public worship—Reformed Church. I. Muether, John R. II. Title.
BX9427 .H37 2002
264'.042—dc21　　　　　　　　　　　　　　　　　　　　2001059342

To
Jay and Ellen Hart
and
Herbert and Anne Muether

Contents

Acknowledgments

This book began as a series of Sunday school lessons, delivered by each author in his respective congregation of the Orthodox Presbyterian Church (OPC). We are grateful to the sessions of Lake Sherwood OPC in Orlando, Florida, and Calvary OPC in Glenside, Pennsylvania, for allowing us the opportunity to develop our thoughts about worship in the setting of adult education. Thanks also go to the members of these congregations, who sometimes enjoyed and other times endured our lessons. The book would be inferior without the responses we received at this initial stage.

We are also grateful to the former editors of *The Outlook*, Tom and Laurie Vanden Heuvel, who graciously published most of the material that follows in a slightly revised form. W. Robert Godfrey, then a contributing editor to *The Outlook*, encouraged us to submit the written form of our Sunday school lessons to the Vanden Heuvels, whose enthusiastic support for the project provided encouragement and incentive.

Finally, we would like to acknowledge the important assistance rendered by a number of people who read the book at a later stage and gave useful instructions for improvement. They include Kathy Muether, Ann Hart, Craig and Carol Troxel, Chad and Emily Van Dixhoorn, Grace Mullen, Pat Roach, Marcus and Chandra Mininger, Brent Ferry, Stephen and Lisa Oharek, and Larry Wilson. Of course, none of these people deserves blame for the views in this book that readers find objectionable. Neither do they deserve credit for those ideas deemed particularly penetrating. For all folly and wisdom in this volume not attributed to someone else, the authors take full responsibility.

The book is dedicated to our parents, who instilled in us a sense of the seriousness of what we did collectively with other saints on Sunday mornings. In so doing they gave us our first significant instruction, however informal, in the basics of worship.

Introduction

Sound Doctrine and Worship

What's all the fuss? These days Christians seem to have an easy time starting a fight over worship. Mention that the church's hymnbooks ought to be replaced. Suggest that the elders revise the liturgy. Or raise a question over the celebration of Christmas. And responses reveal that *worship* has become a fighting word. Reformed Christians, staunchly united on the God they confess, able to articulate the "solas" of the Reformation and the five points of Calvinism, are increasingly divided over how they ought to worship their God.

If you listen carefully to current debates, you will encounter rhetoric that is strange for Reformed Christians. Here are some comments we have heard, none of which is terribly unusual:

+ "I like a church that is casual, where I know I can go and relax during worship."
+ "I don't always enjoy my church's worship, but that's okay. I know it'll be different next week."
+ "I'm tired of the barrenness of worship—I'm looking for something with more beauty."

- ✦ "Worship is ultimately a matter of taste, and there's no accounting for that."
- ✦ "If there is one thing you can say about our worship, it's not boring!"

These popular sentiments all remind us that there is significant confusion about the nature, purpose, and practice of worship. This confusion extends to the Reformed community, and it underscores the urgency of recovering a biblical view of worship.

"Worship wars" is how some have labeled the battles that often result in congregational worship committees replacing organs with guitars, hymnals with overheads, pulpits with stages. How ought we to evaluate these innovations in our churches? What do we expect from worship? How do we judge good worship from bad? Is there even such a thing as bad worship? How would we recognize it?

And how did we get to this place? After all, Reformed Protestants are agreed on our chief end—to glorify God and enjoy him forever. We also agree about the importance of doctrine and hold to the same system of theology, one that makes God sovereign in redemption and gives him all glory. So how can we differ so much on right worship? Our calling to glorify God may be too often colored by other assumptions. For example, many believe that the *sincerity* and *informality* of the worship experience is the chief barometer of good worship. Because we think we are more sincere when we are spontaneous and liberated from restraint, we are tempted to conclude that informal, casual worship frees the emotions and that formality or restraint represses our emotions. Somehow we can't enjoy God if we can't offer up all of our emotions, including our desire to be casual. The problem with this thinking arises when we consider how easily our feelings can fool us. We can all too easily fake sincerity and zeal. What is more, we are fallen and do not always feel the proper emotions. So by themselves, emotions serve as no standard.

Another common assumption has to do with evangelism. Evangelism is an important calling of the church, and we ought to yearn to see new converts. So let's remove the barriers that keep unchurched Harry and Mary away, some say, and make worship more user friendly. But ought the standard for the public gathering of God's people in his presence be those of the unbeliever? Where does the Bible encourage us to design worship for outsiders?

These and other assumptions are derailing us from the task of glorifying God in worship. We need to return to basics on worship. That is the purpose of this little book. On the basis of Scripture and Reformed confessions, we have designed a primer on what is arguably the Christian's most important calling. A primer is defined as a short, introductory book on a single subject. This is exactly what follows—a brief overview of how Reformed theology informs the way we think about, put together, and participate in a worship service. Our aim is to help church officers and members gather corporately for worship and do so in ways appropriate to the God who has revealed himself in Christ Jesus.

Theology Matters

We begin from an explicitly Reformed perspective, because worship inevitably follows from theological conviction. As the apostle Paul wrote to Titus, certain things are "fitting for sound doctrine," matters such as temperateness, dignity, sensibleness, faith, love, and perseverance (Titus 2:1–2). So too we believe that good theology must produce good worship, corporate acts of praise and devotion that fit the sound theology of the Reformed tradition. On the other hand, defective theology yields inferior or inappropriate forms of worship. The Protestant Reformers understood this. The confessions of the sixteenth and seventeenth centuries were all aimed at reforming the worship of the church. For example, the Westminster divines did not merely write a confession and catechisms, but started with the *Directory for the Public Worship of*

God before completing the Westminster Standards. Because of the close connection between good theology and appropriate worship, corporate acts of praise and devotion that conflict with Reformed theology must flow from unsound doctrine. In effect, our worship provides a barometer of our theology.

Consequently, if we are self-consciously Reformed, our worship will embody our confessional commitments in particular ways. As Reformed Protestants we will likely worship differently from non-Reformed Christians. For example, Calvinists will give liturgical expression to the Creator-creature distinction (a doctrine not unique to Calvinism, yet one given fuller attention in Calvinism than in other traditions). The vast gulf separating God from his creation means that God alone is infinite and independent, and that we are finite and dependent. This will restrain the notions of individualism, self-confidence, and assertiveness that our culture privileges. Instead, humility and self-denial will characterize our comportment.

Calvinists also stress the doctrine of divine sovereignty, or the idea that God is Lord over all things. He may do with his creation as he pleases. His "rights" are limited only by his own character, his wisdom, power, holiness, justice, goodness, and truth. The implications for worship are obvious. Worship is pleasing to God when it acknowledges his absolute claims upon his creation, and when believers do not presume, either explicitly or implicitly in their actions and attitudes in worship, to question his sovereignty. In other words, Reformed worship must be explicitly theocentric. If not, if it tends to be directed toward pleasing man, whether believers or unbelievers, then it has lost the Reformed conviction that God, his ways, and his Word must shape our service of worship.

Another doctrine of the Reformed tradition is total depravity. The mind, the will, the affections—all are corrupted by sin. Nothing that we can do by ourselves can please God. This means that we are incapable by our own intelligence, strength, or sincerity of devising God-honoring worship. This is a depressing view to many and appears to deny the genuine beauty and wisdom that men and women create through their God-given abilities. Still, Reformed Christians have historically felt the weight of this claim and have approached worship accordingly. They have not assumed that whatever they do to worship God, no matter how well intended, is pleasing to him. Scripture, in fact, testifies to precisely the reverse. When Cain presented an offering to God of fruit and vegetables (Gen. 4:3), he might have appeared to act out of genuine devotion. But God was not pleased with Cain's sacrifice. Instead, he "had regard" for Abel's sacrifice of meat (Gen. 4:4). For this reason Calvinists have been particularly committed to the principle that true worship must conform to the Bible, to what God has revealed as being acceptable to him. As John Calvin himself observed, human nature is a "perpetual factory of idols."[1]

Soundness in doctrine, then, goes hand-in-hand with what is appropriate in worship. Historically, Reformed worship has always flowed from Reformed theology. Simply put, you can't have one without the other. If our worship differs markedly from the ways in which Reformed believers have worshiped in the past, then there is a good chance that our theology, though apparently unchanged, no longer governs our corporate worship.

We recognize that some in the Reformed camp may be troubled by the connection we are drawing between theology and worship. It is not uncommon to hear people express a desire to see theology quarantined to the sermon. "As long as the sermon is theologically accurate," the argument goes, "whatever you do in the rest of the service is okay." But this way of thinking has dangerous implications. Would we restrict the lordship of Christ in other areas of life, as if God's sovereignty applies only to politics but not to marriage? Even more striking, why do we seem more concerned these days about a Reformed worldview in economics or art but take a more relaxed view when it comes to worship? And if our theology does not shape our worship, then what about the Lordship of Christ over all areas of life? In other words, why try so hard to act Reformed six days of the week but let up on the first and holy day? Why refuse to practice what we bother to profess?

This connection between theology and worship is so vital that it is impossible to change the form (worship practice) without altering the content (theological conviction). Certainly our theological standards make no such distinction. Even though the Westminster divines wrote a separate directory for worship, for instance, the Westminster Confession is not silent about the proper way to worship. Chapter 21 speaks of the reading of the Word "with godly fear," "sound preaching, and conscionable hearing of the word, . . . with understanding, faith, and reverence," the singing of psalms, the administration and reception of the sacraments "instituted by Christ," and prayers "made for things lawful" (21.5, 4). Likewise the Belgic Confession says that the marks of a true church are visible during worship. "If the pure doctrine of the gospel is preached" and if the church maintains "the pure administration of the sacraments as instituted by Christ," then you know the church is Reformed according to the Word (art. 29). The Reformers assumed correct theological content would express itself in worship, that is, in proper forms. Being Reformed, then, means more than holding to a certain system of doctrine or a certain kind of church government. It also involves certain practices, and some of the most important of these activities take place in public worship.

We suggest that when churches undergo dramatic changes in what is often called "worship style," they may actually be changing their theology as well. Form and content cannot be separated. So in congregations where worship has changed, something significant may have happened also to their theology. Is it possible to preach the whole counsel of God in an up-tempo service? Can the hard truths of Calvinism be taught in a setting geared toward attracting outsiders? Can pointing out our sinfulness ever be made appealing? Churches that depart from older patterns of worship may very well abandon the theological coherence assumed by the

Reformed creeds and confessions. When this coherence is lost, something must replace it. In our day the solution comes either through evangelistic zeal that makes soul-winning the sole criterion for evaluating the ministry of the church, or through therapeutic forms of positive reinforcement that orient worship more toward self-fulfillment than to self-denial.

Worship and Language

We need to say a word here about language, the vocabulary we use to talk about worship. Language both shapes and reflects our behavior. Throughout our study we will examine how Christians tend to talk when reflecting on worship.

Consider, for example, the use of the term *worship experience*. This phrase threatens to eclipse the older expression, *worship service*. What difference does it make? We believe the difference is enormous. Service is the work and duty of a servant to and for a superior, and good service is that which pleases the superior. The word *experience* redirects the goal of worship, from God-centeredness to man's pleasure. We become the audience or the consumer, and our criteria for good worship shift. Good worship must excite, exhilarate, and even entertain us; in turn, bad worship is joyless, monotonous, and above all, boring—the word to end all debate.

Another revealing word is *celebration*. This word has a venerable history in worship, as when churches "celebrate" the Lord's Supper. But what happens when the meaning is altered, when celebration suggests the high-fiving, champagne-spraying swagger of World Series champions or the exuberant and raucous festivities on New Year's Eve at Times Square? Of course there are other kinds of celebration, such as the dignity and gravity of a king's coronation or the simple solemnity of a church wedding. We must be mindful of these differences and not sanction by our language certain forms of celebration that are inappropriate for the church gathered for worship.

And does it matter that the sermon is now frequently called a "message"? *Message* sounds softer, less threatening, and more accessible. It may have the effect of turning the speaker into one of us, a regular guy whose effectiveness is measured by how well he relates to his audience by using humor and engaging illustrations. This image seems far removed from the voice of God delivered by his servant, a steward of divine mysteries, who must handle the word of truth with utmost care.

So language is important, and we want to reflect carefully on the words we use in worship. Ecclesiastes reads: "Guard your steps as you go to the house of God and draw near to listen rather than to offer the sacrifice of fools. . . . Do not be hasty in word or impulsive in thought to bring up a matter in the presence of God. For God is in heaven and you are on the earth; therefore let your words be few" (Eccles. 5:1–2). Although the author of Ecclesiastes mixes good and bad advice until the final chapter, clearly this is good advice. Our silence and words in worship require careful attention. We need to watch our tongues lest we offer the "sacrifice of fools."

Outlining Our Study

At this point readers may be tempted to think: good theology and precise language are well and good, but let's cut to the chase — what about dance and skits? What's wrong with praise choruses? How about guitars and overheads? This book may frustrate those looking for answers to such questions because we do not intend to give immediate answers to the debates surrounding contemporary worship. In our view the current controversies have much to do with more basic issues. These fundamental concerns are as much contested as the specific matters of music, dance, and drama. We are convinced that one can only think through the specific examples of contemporary practice after reflecting on more preliminary and primary matters.

First, *who* is it that worships? Our consideration of worship must first look at the church as the community gathered for worship. In other words, a proper ecclesiology is necessary for understanding worship. It is no coincidence that contemporary confusion about worship is occurring when there is so much misunderstanding about the church of Christ.

Another important question is *when* to worship. Here we will look at the doctrine of the Sabbath and how it informs our worship practice. What does it mean to set apart the first day of the week? Worshiping God appropriately is directly connected to the sanctification of the Lord's Day. This is why, for example, the Westminster Confession teaches about the Sabbath in chapter 21 on worship. Keeping the Lord's Day holy is the foundation for understanding the place of corporate worship in the Christian life.

After considering who worships and when, we turn to a series of *how* questions. What is the "regulative principle" and how does it guide us in worship? What is the "dialogical principle" and how does it shape our liturgy? Who leads in worship and how does the congregation meaningfully participate in the service? What is the proper attitude for worship—how do you worship with reverence *and* joy? What is the place in worship of the means of grace? What are the elements of worship and how do they differ from circumstances?

Finally we take up what is arguably the most controversial topic in worship debates: music. Unfortunately this is often where controversy starts. But we want to cover it at the end after these other matters, so that we treat congregational song in the proper context. By presenting the material this way, we hope that much of the acrimony can be both clarified and diffused. After examining the role of song in worship, we suggest ways in which Reformed Christians should exercise discernment, distinguishing the good from the bad, the true from the false, and biblical worship from blasphemy.

Throughout we will explore the Scriptures along with our Reformed confessions. We will try to do justice to the reverence the Psalmist expressed when he despaired over the holiness required to enter into God's presence: "Who may ascend into the hill of the LORD? And who may stand in His holy place? He who has clean hands and a pure heart, who has not lifted up his soul to falsehood and has not sworn deceitfully" (Ps. 24:3–4). The Bible's demand that worshipers be holy and pure means that our confidence in worship comes only from Christ. As the author of Hebrews put it, "Therefore let us draw near with confidence to the throne of grace, so that we may receive mercy and find grace to help in time of need" (Heb. 4:16). These mutual demands for purity and confidence in worship help to explain the biblical idea of rejoicing "with trembling" (Ps. 2:11). The Bible regards reverence and joy not as opposites that we turn on and off during worship, but as mutually reinforcing, just as the death and resurrection of Christ nurture both humility and celebration. The Old Testament still informs Christian worship. Contrary to much popular thinking, God has not lowered his standards for Israel's worship to those now in place for the church. Throughout redemptive history, God despises false worship. The fire that consumed Nadab and Abihu (Lev. 10:1–7) still consumes false worshipers today (Heb. 12:22–29).

Recovering Reformed Worship

This primer will not be exhaustive. It is a place to begin to think through the implications of Reformed theology for how we worship. Even less do we claim that this primer's contents will prove immediately agreeable in all its assertions. Sociologists note that we live in postconfessional and anti-intellectual times. American Protestants today have abandoned denominational traditions, opting instead for a blended or generic spirituality and worship. Methodists, Baptists, Presbyterians, and even Catholics are less dis-

cernibly so in the ways they conduct themselves in worship. Without denominational loyalty or creedal constraints, so-called "new
paradigm" churches are reinventing worship by developing popular and seeker-oriented "styles." These innovations cast aside a
well-defined piety of the past in the interests of excitement,
dynamic spirituality, and relevance.

Although some applaud this transformation as a kind of ecu-
menical breakthrough, we fear that the decline of distinctively
Reformed habits of worship is not a sign of greater tolerance but
an indication that many in the Reformed camp no longer see the
implications of their theology for their worship services. Recovering the practices of Reformed worship, we concede, will be difficult. But many Presbyterians and Reformed have not let the
changes in American Protestantism affect their attachment to
Reformed theology. For this loyalty we are thankful. Our task is to
show that such faithfulness to Reformed doctrine also requires loyalty to a certain kind of worship. To put it differently, holding on
to the content of the Reformed faith also involves adhering to the
practices and forms of Reformed worship.

Nevertheless, North American Calvinists have never been
known for winning popularity contests. Calvinism does not have
the reputation of empowering or affirming those who are faint of
theological heart. Ironically, however, there is a sense in which
what we propose in this study is profoundly seeker-sensitive. We
do not mean that we hope to please any browsers who might step
into our sanctuaries on Sunday morning. Rather the seeker we
intend to please is the one whom Scripture describes as the seeker
of acceptable worship. In his conversation with the Samaritan
woman, Jesus says that those who worship God in spirit and truth
are the kind of worshipers "the Father seeks" (John 4:23). This is
the seeker-sensitivity that the Bible requires and that Reformed
worship has traditionally pursued.

One last reminder concerns the importance of our subject. The
worship of God is the most fundamental aspect of Christian duty.

We were created to serve God, and our worship on the Lord's Day should be conducted to give him the glory and honor that belong to him alone as our Creator, Redeemer, and Sustainer. The Ten Commandments, after all, begin with four commandments that have everything to do with worship. If some would desire a greater adherence to God's law in modern societies, what better way to begin than by making sure that our churches follow God's requirements for worship? Without a proper understanding and practice of worship, we run the risk of failing to obey what Christ called "the great and foremost commandment" (Matt. 22:39).

1

The Church
and the World

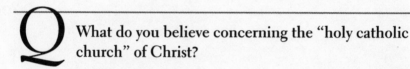

Q What do you believe concerning the "holy catholic church" of Christ?

A That the Son of God from the beginning to the end of the world, gathers, defends, and preserves to Himself by His Spirit and Word, out of the whole human race, a Church chosen to everlasting life, agreeing in true faith; and that I am and for ever shall remain, a living member thereof.

(Heidelberg Catechism, 54)

What is the relationship between the church and the world in worship? Should the service be a time that makes the church accessible to the world, or should it be one where the church displays her otherworldliness? Should worship be a means to attract the unchurched to the gospel, or should it be an expression of the church's identity as aliens and strangers in the world?

The answer to these questions used to be fairly easy. J. Gresham Machen, who battled worldliness in the church through his whole life, had little trouble defending the idea that the church should be separate from the world. In "The Separateness of the Church," a sermon he preached at Princeton Seminary in 1925 on Matthew 5:13 ("You are the salt of the earth. . . ."), Machen declared that these words of Christ "established at the very beginning the distinctness and separateness of the Church." If the distinction between the church and the world was ever lost, Machen warned, "the power of the Church is gone. The Church then becomes like salt that has lost its savor, and is fit only to be cast out and to be trodden under foot of men."[1]

The antithesis that Machen recognized as basic to the Bible's teaching about the church prompted him to oppose all the concessions that liberal Protestants were making to the wisdom of the world. In an effort to retain the truth of Christianity in the face of scientific discoveries that made the gospel incredible to college-educated people, liberal Protestantism had reduced Christianity to the seemingly safe and reassuring truths of the Golden Rule and the Sermon on the Mount. But the effort to maintain the church's credibility had resulted in a worldly church, like salt that had lost

25

its savor. Machen believed that if the church were faithful to the Great Commission she could not let the wisdom of the world obscure both the power and foolishness of the cross.

Conservative Presbyterian and Reformed folk throughout the twentieth century believed with Machen that the antithesis between the church and the world was a good thing. But that no longer appears to be the case. With liberalism no longer the threat that it was in the 1920s, our churches seem to be more concerned about winning the approval of the world and less on guard against the dangers of conforming to the world. What is more, with fundamentalism carrying the negative associations of intolerance and bigotry, many Reformed and Presbyterians try to avoid doing or saying things that might be construed as narrow-minded or sectarian. Instead, in an effort to reach out to the unchurched, some congregations are more willing to reconsider certain forms of worldliness. If the church looks more normal, the logic goes, then it may look more attractive to outsiders.

What Is the Church?

Q&A 54 from the Heidelberg Catechism is a good place to begin a consideration of the separateness of the church. It pictures God as the actor in salvation, who is gathering a people for himself from the ends of the earth. The church is a people called out of the world into fellowship with their God. The very word for church, *ekklēsia* in the Greek, means "called out," and it describes the relocation involved in salvation. We have left behind our old identity to embrace a new one in Christ. The same point holds for worship. We leave the world and its cares and duties to enter into God's presence.

This Greek word, *ekklēsia*, is the translation of the Hebrew word *qahal*, which means "assembly." But more is intended than a mere gathering of people. Israel was the Old Testament assembly of the people of God. In the Exodus, God had taken a chosen people, a gathered people, out of the world (Egypt) and brought them to himself at Mount Sinai. Israel was an assembly at Sinai because the people were gathered in the presence of God. In Deuteronomy we read, "Assemble the people to Me, that I may let them hear My words so that they may learn to fear Me all the days they live on the earth, and that they may teach their children" (Deut. 4:10). To assemble the people of God is to have them stand before the Lord.

In the New Testament, the church becomes the assembly of God's people. The author of Hebrews draws the parallel between the worship of the church and the assembly of the Israelites at Sinai in the following manner:

> For you have not come to a mountain that can be touched and to a blazing fire, and to darkness and gloom and whirlwind. . . . But you have come to Mount Zion and to the city of the living God, the heavenly Jerusalem, and to myriads of angels, to the general assembly and church of the firstborn who are enrolled in heaven, and to God, the Judge of all, and to the spirits of the righteous [men] made perfect. . . . (Heb. 12:18, 22–23).

Just as Israel was called out of Egypt to Sinai, so the church is the gathering of God's people, out of the world and into fellowship with God. The church at worship is therefore an assembly that is separate from the world, because it is God who separates the church, in order to gather with him, to be in his presence.

To be a church, an *ekklēsia*, requires being separate from the world. The church cannot gather in the presence of God if it is still in the world. For this reason Paul describes the separateness of the church in strong language:

> Do not be bound together with unbelievers; for what partnership have righteousness and lawlessness, or what fel-

lowship has light with darkness? Or what harmony has
Christ with Belial, or what has a believer in common with
an unbeliever? Or what agreement has the temple of God
with idols? For we are the temple of the living God; just as
God said, "I will dwell in them and walk among them; and
I will be their God, and they shall be My people. There-
fore, come out from their midst and be separate," says the
Lord. (2 Cor. 6:14–17)

Salvation involves a new identity, which finds expression in our
joining the church, that is, the people of God's possession.

What Is the World?

Fundamentalism may have given the notion of being separate
from worldliness a bad name, but most Christians who read the
Bible understand that God requires some form of renunciation
from those who follow Christ. What, then, should the separateness of the church look like in worship? In other words, what is
the world that we must leave behind when we gather for worship?

The Bible describes the world in three senses. It can refer simply to the created order, as in Acts: "The God who made the world
and all things in it, since He is Lord of heaven and earth, does not
dwell in temples made with hands" (Acts 17:24). It can refer also
to the nations of the earth, the human race, the world that God
will judge. For instance, the apostle Paul raises the question of
whether God's wrath is in some way unrighteous and responds:
"May it never be! For otherwise, how will God judge the world?"
(Rom. 3:6). David Wells argues that it is appropriate for the church
to be worldly in these two senses of the term: we are to be good
stewards of God's creation, and we are to show love for our neighbors by taking the gospel *into the world,* to the whole human race,
to the ends of the earth. The Bible clearly teaches that separation
from the world in these ways is forbidden. Jesus prays to his father

that we not be taken from the world, because he has sent us into
the world: "I do not ask You to take them out of the world, but to
keep them from the evil one. . . . As You sent Me into the world,
I also have sent them into the world" (John 17:15, 18).

Scripture goes on to refer to the world in a third sense, the world
as fallen humanity in rebellion against God. In Wells's words this
is "the collective expression of every society's refusal to bow before
God, to receive his truth, to obey his commandments, or to believe
in his Christ."[2] The *world* in this sense is also that way of life that
fallen humanity substitutes for God's holy ways. It is the world as
an idol, as a rival to God's Word, "their appetites, the way that they
order their life, their priorities, their behavior, what they really
want, and what they will do to get it."[3] This is how Christ prayed
as a high priest in John: "I glorified You on the earth, having accom-
plished the work which You have given Me to do. Now, Father,
glorify Me together with Yourself, with the glory which I had with
You before the world was" (John 17:4–5). Here the *world* refers to
something of which Christ was not a part; nor should his people
belong to the world in this sense. What is more, this world was the
one for which Christ refused to pray. Just a few verses later, Christ
prayed, "I do not ask on behalf of the world" (John 17:9).

It is this sense of worldliness that must inform the church's otherworldliness. The Bible calls Christians strangers in this world.
Peter writes, "Peter, an apostle of Jesus Christ, to those who reside
as aliens, scattered throughout Pontus, Galatia, Cappadocia, Asia,
and Bithynia" (1 Peter 1:1). If he were writing today he would
have referred to those Christian exiles living in Nigeria, Japan,
Serbia, Canada, and Brazil. Wherever Christians live they do so
as "aliens and strangers" (1 Peter 2:11), because, in the words of
the writer to the Hebrews, ". . . they desire a better country, that
is, a heavenly one. Therefore God is not ashamed to be called
their God; for He has prepared a city for them" (Heb. 11:16). In
this sense the church and the world have nothing to do with each
other. The church is *contra mundum*, against the world. As strange

as it sounds, we are to hate the world and the things of the world. As Christ himself said, "If anyone comes to Me, and does not hate his own father and mother and wife and children and brothers and sisters, yes, and even his own life, he cannot be My disciple" (Luke 14:26).

Holiness versus Worldliness

In his sermon on the "Separateness of the Church," Machen observed that "the real threat to the church has always come from within, not without." This internal threat is deadly precisely because it denies the separateness of the church by gradually merging the church with the world under the guise of peace. An "all embracing paganism" results, Machen warned, when the church forsakes its call to holiness and pursues worldliness.[4]

When Christians recite the Apostles' Creed, they say they believe "in the *holy* Catholic church." What does the holiness of the church mean? Peter links holiness with the idea of gathering: "But you are a chosen race, a royal priesthood, a holy nation, a people for God's own possession, so that you may proclaim the excellencies of Him who has called you out of darkness into His marvelous light" (1 Peter 2:9). To be holy, in other words, is to be called and gathered by the Holy One as his treasured possession. Sometimes Scripture describes this holiness in an objective or ceremonial sense (such as the tabernacle and the priests, who were holy because they were set apart for the worship of God), and sometimes in a subjective or ethical sense (such as the infusion of holiness through God's work of sanctification). To be holy, then, means that we are not worldly, because we are set apart from the world. As Paul teaches, ". . . do not be conformed to this world, but be transformed by the renewing of your mind. ..." (Rom. 12:2).

But what exactly is worldliness? For many Christians, worldliness refers to certain forms of amusement, such as playing cards, drinking alcohol, smoking tobacco, or going to movies. Others may think of worldliness as sexual immorality—adultery and divorce, for example. R. B. Kuiper, however, warned that worldliness was not so easily identified. "Few Christians seem to realize," he wrote, "that a church may take a strong stand against certain flagrant sins of the world and yet be decidedly worldly." He added that there "are churches which pride themselves on their firm stand against worldliness and yet want to be great as the world counts greatness. They think in terms of costly stone edifices rather than lively stones that are built up as a spiritual house (1 Peter 2:5). They strive after statistical rather than spiritual prosperity. That also is worldliness."[5]

Kuiper's point is that to think like the world is to be guilty of worldliness. It is not enough to be devoted to the church's prosperity. If we measure the work of the church in worldly terms, such as material wealth or numerical size or programs for all ages, then the church has become like the world. Scripture commands us to see with the eyes of the Spirit, not the eyes of the flesh. This is partly what the apostle Paul had in mind when he wrote that "we look not at the things which are seen, but at the things which are not seen; for the things which are seen are temporal, but the things that are not seen are eternal" (2 Cor. 4:18). It was this truth that prompted Machen to say to the graduates of Westminster Seminary in 1931:

> You, as ministers of Christ, are called to deal with the unseen things. You are stewards of the mysteries of God. You alone can lead men, by the proclamation of God's Word, out of the crash and jazz and noise and rattle and smoke of this weary age into the green pastures and beside the still waters; you alone, as ministers of reconciliation, can give what the world with all its boasting and pride can never give—the infinite sweetness of the communion of the redeemed soul with the living God.[6]

The church is as different from the world as green pastures and still waters are from the cacophony of a weary age. The church's ways are not the world's ways. And that is because God has called the church to be holy as he is holy. He has gathered the church as his assembly. The church is set apart to serve God.

The Church against the World

The biblical distinction drawn so far between holiness and worldliness means that the church is by nature antithetical to the world. The church is at war with the world, and it has the duty to fight worldliness, a duty that we find throughout redemptive history.

With the first promise of a redeemer in Genesis, God announced that all of history, from that point forward, would witness a cosmic battle between two camps. God declared, ". . . I will put enmity between you [the serpent] and the woman, and between your seed and her seed; he shall bruise you on the head, and you shall bruise him on the heel" (Gen. 3:15). The seed of the woman is the church, which is pitted against the seed of the serpent, that is, the world. The battle in view here is of an absolute spiritual antithesis between those chosen for life and those dead in sin, between the children of light and the children of darkness.

Likewise, when Israel crossed the Jordan, the conquest was the cry of holy war, and God called upon Israel to annihilate her enemies. The holy people of God were forbidden to live in peaceful coexistence with their redeemer's enemies. In the New Testament this antithesis becomes a spiritual warfare, as opposed to a physical or national one like Israel's. The church battles the "spiritual forces of wickedness" (Eph. 6:12). In this warfare the world's aim is to crucify Christ and persecute his church, as Jesus himself predicted: "If you were of the world, the world would love its own; but because you are not of the world, but I chose you out of the world, because of this the world hates you. . . . If they persecuted Me, they will also persecute you. ..." (John 15:19–20). Because of this antithesis between the church and the world, R. B. Kuiper concluded that "to be the opposite of the world is not only necessary for the well-being of the church but is essential to its very being. If the church should cease being antithetical to the world, it would no longer be the church."[7] The church today needs to be willing to accept the terms of the antithesis laid down by Christ. God's people, whether they know it or not, are at enmity with the world. This antithesis requires the church to be prepared for combat and to withstand the temptation to conform to the world. It means that the church must renounce the ways of the city of man and follow the laws of the city of God.

This is not to deny that Christians must love their neighbors. Indeed, the antithesis between the church and the world does not contradict what Christ called the second "great" commandment: "You shall love your neighbor as yourself" (Matt. 22:39). Still, such love of neighbor does not refute the fundamental difference between the church and the world, between the ways of God's people and the ways of God's enemies. The church that is faithful to her holy calling will look and act differently from the world.

Unapologetic Worship

What does this have to do with worship? Perhaps the connection is not immediately obvious. One implication is that if the church is at war with the world, the wisdom and ways of the gospel will appear foolish to those who are enemies of God. As Paul writes, "For the word of the cross is foolishness to those who are perishing, but to us who are being saved it is the power of God" (1 Cor. 1:18). Another implication is that the contrast between the church and world will be most obvious when the church is at worship. The church in worship should be like that described by Paul in 1 Thessalonians, that is, turning "from idols to serve a living and true God" (1 Thess. 1:9). The very act of worship, of assembling in the presence of God, therefore, is simultaneously the church's renunciation of the world. Worship is a subversive and counter-cultural act of an alien people who, forsaking the world, listen to the voice of her master saying, "follow me."

True worship, then, will be odd and perhaps even weird to the watching world. This oddness is not lamentable but essential to the church's faithfulness and witness. For if the gospel is foolishness, it is foolish only to those who do not believe. The church may use a human tongue as its language of worship, it may use worldly time to determine when to meet for worship, it may even use electricity drawn from state-run utilities to heat the building and amplify the minister's voice. But when the church assembles for worship she is not at all like the world. She invokes the name of Christ. She prays and sings to a God who cannot be seen. She hears words said by a man commissioned by Christ that become, by the work of the Holy Spirit, the power of God unto salvation. She eats a holy meal whose portions are tiny, but which, by the blessing of Christ, nourishes God's people for eternal life. In all these ways the church at worship is different from the world. All elements of worship look weak and foolish to those outside the house of God. But to God's people they are manna that sustains for eternal life.

For this reason, the church must be unapologetic in her worship. She must not cater to those bound to ridicule her ways as foolish. Christian worship is, in fact, a bold political act. It subverts the world's values by assigning glory and praise to the one whom the world despises. And as weak as the church at worship might appear to the watching world, the truth is that the powers of this world are no match for the power of God who is present among his people when they gather to sing praise, pray, and hear his Word. Moreover the church must reject the claim that worship is old-fashioned, irrelevant, and isolated from the "real world." For believers, the church at worship *is* the real world. The gathering of the saints in the holy of holies is the eschatological foretaste of the new heavens and the new earth, the reality to which all of history is headed.

Of course, visitors to our churches should receive help in finding Joel in the Bible or knowing when to sit or stand. No one
objects to this kind of sensitivity. But the world is predisposed to
misunderstand the church. Christians cannot expect unbelievers
to be comfortable in services of worship that are alien to the ways
of the world. "User-friendly" or "seeker-sensitive" worship is not
an option for the people of God. In fact, worship that demonstrates
the separateness of the church is what Machen called "merciful
unkindness" because it testifies to the world of the hope that is
within us.[8] If the world mocks us, so be it. True worship is for the
church, not for the world.

2

The Purpose
of the Church

Q What is the task of the church?

A And Jesus came up and spoke to them, saying, "All authority has been given to Me in heaven and on earth. Go therefore and make disciples of all the nations, baptizing them in the name of the Father and the Son and the Holy Spirit, teaching them to observe all that I commanded you."

(Matt. 28:18–20)

In the previous chapter we argued that the church must self-consciously assume a posture antithetical to the world. The irony is that the church only bears witness to the world as she resists worldliness, flees idolatry, and hates the deeds of sinful men. How complete does this otherworldliness of the church need to be? What kind of responsibility does the church have to the world? In other words, does the church's hostility to the world mean she has no obligation to those outside her fellowship? Or is part of her mission to those outside the church?

To ask these questions is to explore the purpose of the church. Though evangelicals have made Rick Warren's *The Purpose Driven Church* a Christian bestseller,[1] they remain confused about the church's purpose. One need only look at a story in *Christianity Today* for confirmation. In a listing of "100 Things the Church Is Doing Right," the magazine featured a wide range of Christian good works, from collecting underwear for the homeless to providing automobile maintenance for single women. Among the "ministries" profiled, less than a quarter actually involved the institutional church, and only a handful involved the preaching of the Word.[2] Instead, these churches offered full-service, "seven-days-a-week" sets of activities for all ages and interest groups. Such all-purpose churches call into question the very existence of smaller churches whose simple one-day-a-week ministries can hardly compete with the ecclesiastical Wal-Marts featured in *Christianity Today*.

Reports like this one demonstrate that American Protestantism is divided between competing notions of the purpose of the church. But this competition is not new. It has a long history in the United

States. Some Protestants, for instance, take the view that the church is primarily a tool for the transformation of its culture. In the nineteenth century, New School Presbyterian Albert Barnes articulated this view in the context of the church's relation to social reform. The church, he wrote,

> owes an important duty to society and to God . . . ; and its mission will not be accomplished by securing merely the sanctification of its own members, or even by the drawing within its fold multitudes of those who shall be saved. . . . The burden which is laid upon it may not be primarily the conversion of the heathen or the diffusion of Bibles and tracts abroad; the work which God requires it to do, and for which specifically it has been planted there, may be to diffuse a definite moral influence in respect to an existing evil institution. On all that is wrong in social life, in the modes of intercourse, in the habits of training the young, and in the prevailing sentiments in the community that have grown out of existing institutions, God may have planted the church there to exert a definite moral influence — a work for himself.[3]

Barnes offers a classic description of the church as an agent of social and moral renewal. Conversion and sanctification of sinners was not making enough of a difference. Instead, the primary work of the church was its exercise of social influence. This view would eventually become the basis for the Social Gospel in the latter part of the nineteenth century. One argument that conservative Protestants used against the Social Gospel was that it let the affairs of the world set the church's agenda.

James Henley Thornwell, the Southern Old School Presbyterian and a contemporary of Barnes, articulated an alternative view of the church's responsibility to society:

[The church] is not, as we fear too many are disposed to regard it, a moral institute of universal good, whose business it is to wage war upon every form of human ill, whether social, civil, political, moral, and to patronize every expedient which a romantic benevolence may suggest as likely to contribute to human comfort. . . . The problems which the anomalies of our fallen state are continually forcing on philanthropy, the church has no right directly to solve. She must leave them to providence, and to human wisdom sanctified and guided by the spiritual influences which it is her glory to foster and cherish. The church is a very peculiar society; . . . it is the kingdom of her Lord Jesus Christ. . . . It can hear no voice but His, obey no command but His, pursue no ends but His.[4]

Here is a complete reversal of Barnes's outlook. The world does not set the agenda for the church. Only Christ, the head of the church, establishes its ministry through his Word. The task of the church is to exalt its head, to teach only the doctrines he has revealed, to worship him as he has commanded, and to order its life by what he has ordained. The church is not an agent of social transformation, though it may contribute to it. The purpose of the church is not to save the world, but to save God's people from the world. These two models have vied with each other throughout the history of American Protestantism. Their differences lay at the heart of the New School–Old School division in nineteenth-century Presbyterianism and the modernist-fundamentalist controversy of the twentieth century.

Still a third version of the purpose of the church comes from the church-growth movement in contemporary American evangelicalism. Begun in the 1950s, the church-growth school uses the methods of social science to figure out why some congregations grow and others don't. Its findings have been used by church planters to identify methods of successful church planting. Telemarketing campaigns, spacious and comfortable facilities, contemporary choruses sung to up-tempo music, dramatic skits, warm messages focusing on helping families cope with the pressures of modern life—all of these techniques are employed to draw people who find older styles of worship and church life irrelevant and old-fashioned.

The more candid church planters in this camp will go so far as to compare the church to a business and urge it to adopt a more entrepreneurial mindset. So the successful church will be market driven, seeing the gospel as its product and the local community as the market. According to George Barna, "The more successful a church is at fulfilling people's needs, the greater its chances for growth."[5]

For church-growth proponents, the primary purpose of the church is to attract newcomers. Typically, this is done by "target audience profiles" of a specific age range and socio-economic profile. The task of the church is to make itself attractive to a specific demographic segment. In many congregations, this thinking has prompted the introduction of contemporary worship with dance, skits, and messages that avoid "Christianese" or evangelical jargon that bewilders, scares, or bores the unchurched.

In line with the New School emphasis of Barnes, these churches are trying to get themselves out of their ghetto in order to influence their communities. In the words of one practitioner, they seek to "outgrow the ingrown church." Not in line with the Old School sentiments of Thornwell, these churches are not limiting themselves to the Lord's specific commands. Stressing an "outward face to the world," they are more sensitive to the language of the world than to the vocabulary and grammar of the church.

As different as these three models are, they share in common a commitment to fulfilling the Great Commission. The Great Commission seems to be a simple set of instructions: "Go therefore and make disciples of all the nations, baptizing them in the name of the Father and the Son and the Holy Spirit, teaching them to observe all that I commanded you" (Matt. 28:19–20). But as these competing models of the church make clear, the meaning of Christ's command to his disciples is not at all obvious to believers today. So the Great Commission is where we ought to begin to understand the purpose of the church.

Whose *Commission Is It?*

A large, multimillion-dollar parachurch organization had as its mission the goal "to help give every man, woman, and child in the entire world an opportunity to find new life in Jesus Christ."[6] It based this goal on the Great Commission. Another parachurch organization has produced the *Great Commission Handbook,* which prompted the website GoYe.org. Of course, it is commendable to see Christians expressing a burden for the lost. Yet it is important to underscore that the Great Commission is not given to individuals or to the parachurch. Jesus gave the Great Commission explicitly to his apostles. But since the promise extends beyond the apostolic age, to the end of this age, we must ask, whose commission is it after the time when the apostles ministered? The answer can be found in Matthew 16:17–19, where we find the apostle Peter's confession of Christ, which is the "Great Constitution" of the church. Edmund Clowney writes that these two texts must be understood together: "The Great Commission of Matthew 28 requires the order Christ has appointed for his church in the Constitution of Matthew 16."[7]

Rightly understood, the Great Commission is the task of the church. It follows, then, that the Great Commission is directed specifically to the ministers of the Word. After all, the commission directs us to baptize. The sacrament of baptism is given to the church, to be administered only by her officers. This contradicts the prevailing notion that special office in the church is really unimportant. Frequently office is disparaged in the interest of promoting the "priesthood of believers," and a high view of the church is greeted with the charges of clericalism and elitism, which play well in the North American democratic and egalitarian culture. However, the priesthood of believers doesn't mean that all believers are pastors, and the general office in the church should not swallow up the special offices of minister, elder, and deacon. (See chapter 7 for a fuller discussion.)

As stewards of the mysteries of God, ministers in particular are set apart in the New Covenant for the ministry of Word and sacrament just as priests were in the Old Covenant. John Calvin underscored this point in his Geneva Confession of 1537, explaining that the church should "receive the true ministers of the Word of God as messengers and ambassadors of God," to "hearken" to these ministers as to Christ himself, and to consider "their ministry as a commission from God necessary in the church" (art. 20).

The church is no human invention. God ordained it for the task of the Great Commission that Christ gave to the apostles. For this reason, we can be sure from Scripture that, despite their multi-million-dollar annual budgets, parachurch organizations like the ones described above cannot fulfill their missions. This is because they have usurped tasks that Christ has given to his church. We dare not replace the church with a vehicle of our design, no matter how much more efficient it may seem to operate. Christ offers his heavenly authority and protection only to his church, and only her ministers, Calvin wrote, "might confidently expect to be victorious over the whole world."[8]

What *Is the Church's Commission?*

Another problem surrounding the Great Commission is to mistake it simply as a command to evangelize. With the dawn of the worldwide missionary efforts in the nineteenth century, evangelicals have read Christ's command with an emphasis on the words *go* and *all nations*. The Great Commission becomes in effect a prooftext for both foreign missions and door-to-door evangelism.

In his popular *Outgrowing the Ingrown Church*, C. John Miller sums up the Great Commission in this way: "It is the privilege and duty of each believer to become God's zealous pacesetter in bringing the lost to Christ by every means available."[9] But this understanding reduces the Great Commission to evangelism and further restricts evangelism to spreading information about the gospel to the world and eliciting decisions for Christ. The Great Commission is not only about evangelism, nor is it mainly about evangelism. It is bigger. We must proclaim the gospel to the lost and desire that converts come to Christ. But that is not the only function of the church, and it is certainly not the focus of its worship.

The Great Commission itself suggests something very different. The main verb in the Greek is not *go* (which is a modifying participle), but *disciple* (which is the imperative). The text literally reads, "as you go, disciple, by teaching and baptizing." This points us to the truth that salvation involves far more than conversion. It involves becoming a disciple of Christ. The goal of the church is not to extend the gospel message to everyone or to bring more folks through the doors of our churches. Rather, it should be exactly what Christ commands here: "teaching them to observe everything I have commanded you." This is the aim of the church's ministry.

This is why Thornwell's understanding of the church was so profound. He went on to write:

> [The church] can hear no voice but Christ's, obey no commands but His, pursue no ends but His. Its officers are His servants bound to execute only his will; its doctrines are His teachings, which He as a prophet has given from God; its discipline His law, which He as king has ordained. . . . The church can announce what [the Bible] teaches, enjoin what it commands, prohibit what it condemns, and enforce her testimonies by spiritual sanctions. Beyond the Bible she can never go, and apart from the Bible she can never speak.[10]

Here Thornwell echoed Calvin, who wrote in a similar fashion about the Great Commission:

> Let this be a firm principle: No other word is to be held as the Word of God, and given place as such in the church, than what is contained first in the Law and the Prophets, then in the writings of the apostles; and the only authorized way of teaching in the church is by the prescription and standard of his Word.[11]

In one sense, it might be argued that Calvin and Thornwell held a narrow perspective on the church, limiting what it could do and say. But in another sense, they understood that a huge burden has been placed on the church and that she is the only institution ordained to perform this task. Thornwell and Calvin's zeal to keep the church's mission clear stemmed from their fear of what would happen to the Great Commission if the institution to which it was given failed to do what Christ intended. The church disciples *all* nations by *teaching them everything Christ had commanded.* This involves the whole counsel of God, not the "four spiritual laws" or even the "five points of Calvinism."

What Is Discipleship?

What then is discipleship? To many people it means *assimilation.* This is the process of getting new members more fully involved in the life of the church, whether through Vacation Bible School or small-group Bible studies, singing in the choir, or serving in the nursery. We prefer, however, to use an older phrase — Christian nurture — to describe the process of discipleship. In this sense discipleship means being conformed to the whole counsel of God as it is revealed in his only begotten Son. It trains God's people for good works and sustains them with spiritual food for their pilgrimage in the wilderness of this world. Christian nurture sees salvation not as a momentary occurrence but as a continuous and arduous process, from which all Christians are prone to wander. It acknowledges that God's people are in need of salvation continually, from regeneration until death. In other words, the way to measure discipleship may have less to do with how active one is in the programs of the church than with how effective the people of God are in resisting worldliness.

This understanding of the Great Commission provides an important context for considering worship. The assembly of God's people is not a time to recharge the batteries of all God's people so they can go out during the week and do the real work of the church either through personal evangelism or fellowship in small-group ministries. Instead, worship is essential to the health of every believer. It is a time when Christians are discipled by God's Word as it is preached, as it is signified and sealed in the sacraments, and as it provides the substance of the church's prayers. Worship is not merely wise; it is necessary for discipleship.

Discipling, teaching, and baptizing—together, these elements of the Great Commission describe what the Reformers understood to be the marks of the true church: the preaching of the Word ("teaching . . . all that I commanded you"), the administration of the sacraments ("baptizing them in the name of the Father and the Son and the Holy Spirit"), and the exercise of discipline ("make disciples"). The Great Commission, then, is a description of the true church fulfilling her mandate. The ministries of Word, sacrament, and prayer disciple God's people. This is the ministry that God has promised to bless, when at the end of the Great Commission our Lord said, ". . . and lo, I am with you always, even to the end of the age" (Matt. 28:20).

Contemporary confusion about the Great Commission arises from two fundamental mistakes. The first is an unwillingness to believe God's promise to use the church and things the world considers foolish to accomplish his purpose of reaching the lost. Much of the innovation in worship today reflects a loss of confidence in the promises that God is bound to keep. We don't seem to believe that he has entrusted to the church the ministry of gathering and perfecting the saints, that he will make the preaching of the Word and the administration of the sacraments effectual to salvation, or that he will supply the officers of his church with all that is necessary for them to carry out this work. We tend to think that we, through our wisdom, effort, and good intentions, can make up for the church's weaknesses. The second mistake comes from understanding the church and its worship merely as vehicles for evangelism. The goal and purpose of the church is to make disciples. Evangelism is only part of the commission Christ gave to his church. If we take the church's responsibility to disciple more seriously, we will not tailor our worship to win the approval of the world. Instead of dumbing it down, we need to have our worship wise up. Through worship God disciples his people. Good worship, worship that is faithful to the Great Commission, will not shy away from teaching all that Christ has commanded.

Thus, it is the *church*, and specifically the *church at worship*, that fulfills the Great Commission. She is ministering to God by gathering a people before him in order to offer the sacrifice of praise. She is ministering to the body of Christ by nurturing it through the ordinances of Word and sacrament. And all of this happens before a watching world. It sees the church engaged in an odd ritual, speaking a strange language, worshiping the true and living God, and rejecting the gods of this world.

Unless we see worship from the perspective of the Great Commission, rightly understood, our worship is prone at best to dishonor God, and at worst, to be a form of blasphemy. Just as bad, it will be ineffective. For finally, only worship that honors God, that conforms to what he has commanded, will God use for convincing and converting sinners and for building them up in holiness and comfort (WSC 89). In other words, worship is essential to the task of the church because it is the Christ-commissioned means of discipling the nations.

3

A Worshiping Community

Q What does Christ give to his church in worship?

A Unto this catholic visible church, Christ has given the ministry, oracles, and ordinances of God, for the gathering and perfecting of the saints, in this life, to the end of the world: and does by his own presence and Spirit, according to his promise, make them effectual.

(Westminster Confession of Faith, 25.3)

The argument advanced thus far has been that in order to understand worship, we first need to comprehend the church and the work God gave to her. And to regard properly the institutional church we need to see its otherworldly character. Only then may we rightly see the significance of the Great Commission. But as important as a prior awareness of the church is to understanding worship, we may also say that without a proper regard for worship we will have a flawed conception of the church. This is because worship constitutes the church. Another way of putting this is to say that the things that believers say and do in worship are essential to being a part of the church of God, the household of faith. It is not an overstatement to assert that the function of church membership is to worship God. As the Shorter Catechism eloquently states in answer 1, "Man's chief end is to glorify God and to enjoy him forever." The fall, obviously, made that end impossible without a savior. Redemption restores man to his original purpose, even though this side of glory human worship will always be tainted with sin. And worship, put simply, is nothing more and nothing less than glorifying and enjoying God.

Saved to Worship

If we had any doubt about the centrality of worship for the church, Exodus furnishes us with a poignant reminder of the intimate relationship between corporate worship and the life of the church. Immediately after the Exodus, God through his inspired servant, Moses, interpreted the significance of the Israelites' trek through the Red Sea. Moses led the Israelites in singing the following:

51

> I will sing to the LORD, for He is highly exalted;
> The horse and its rider He has hurled into the sea.
> The LORD is my strength and song,
> And He has become my salvation;
> This is my God, and I will praise Him;
> My father's God, and I will extol Him. (Exod. 15:1–2)

The Israelites rightly responded to their deliverance from the bondage of Egypt with a song of praise to the God of their salvation. Not only did the Exodus elicit an act of worship, but this song of Moses also showed that God had delivered his covenant people so they could worship him. As the nation set off into the wilderness, the Israelites learned that liberation from Egypt was not the end of God's purpose for them. The people were liberated in order to be gathered as God's treasured possession.

> You will bring them and plant them in the mountain of
>   Your inheritance,
> The place, O LORD, which You have made for Your
>   dwelling,
> The sanctuary, O LORD, which Your hands have estab-
>   lished.
> The LORD shall reign forever and ever. (Exod. 15: 17–18)

Here at the end of Moses' song we understand the reason for Israel's deliverance. God brought Moses and the people out of Egypt to plant them on the mountain of his inheritance, a reference to Mt. Zion, the place where the Temple would one day be erected. In other words, God's people were gathered out of Egypt (the world) in order to be brought into his temple (the place of worship where God was present). The purpose of salvation, then, is worship. The Exodus was the means, and gathering in worship was the end.

The same pattern is true in the New Testament but is heightened because of the mediatorial work of Christ. In the Old Testament only the priest could pass through the outer rooms of the Temple into the holiest of places, the Holy of Holies. As Psalm 24 says, "Who may ascend into the hill of the LORD? And who may stand in His holy place? He who has clean hands and a pure heart, who has not lifted up his soul to falsehood and has not sworn deceitfully" (24:3–4). But now thanks to the finished work of Christ, all who trust in him may enter into the Holy of Holies to give him glory and praise. Paul writes in Colossians that Christ has reconciled us "in order to present [us] before Him holy and blameless and beyond reproach" (1:22). This is why the writer of Hebrews tells the New Testament church that in worship we go to "Mount Zion and to the city of the living God, the heavenly Jerusalem" (Heb. 12:22). The holiness that the church now experiences because of Christ's saving work is further emphasized by the metaphor that Paul uses in 2 Corinthians to describe the church as "the temple of the living God" (6:16). The purpose of salvation is worship because worship is what the people of God are called to do.

The Marks of the Church

Another way of illustrating how worship constitutes the church is to consider the marks of the church. The doctrine of the marks of the church is indeed precious to Protestants because it asserts fundamental differences between Roman Catholicism and the Protestant Reformation. By the marks of the church, according to the Belgic Confession, we can discern the true from the false church. The Belgic Confession goes on to define the marks of the church in the following manner:

> The marks by which the true Church is known are these: if the pure doctrine of the gospel is preached therein; if she maintains the pure administration of the sacraments as instituted by Christ; if church discipline is exercised in

chastening of sin; in short, if all things are managed according to the pure Word of God, all things contrary thereto
rejected, and Jesus Christ acknowledged as the only Head
of the Church. Hereby the true Church may certainly be
known, from which no man has a right to separate himself
(art. 29).

The marks of the church indicate where the true church may be
found. Wherever we see and hear preaching, the sacraments, and
church discipline truly performed, we know we are in the presence of the true church.

    It is important to notice that the marks of the church are bound
up with corporate worship. One might even summarize the doctrine of the marks of the church by saying that the true church can
only be found when she is at worship. Of course, the preaching of
the Word and the administration of baptism and the Lord's Supper
are obviously central parts of worship. Worship is where ministers
preach the Word and administer the sacraments. Discipline is
harder to discern in corporate worship since the believers who
gather on the Lord's Day for worship do so not as a court of the
church (consistory, session, classis, or presbytery) but rather as a
congregation. Still, preaching itself is a form of discipline, in its
manifestation of the ministerial and declarative power of the
church. For Protestants, the keys of the kingdom to which Christ
refers (Matt. 16:18–19; 18:18), are not the basis for Roman Catholic
teaching on papal superiority but rather divine sanction for the holy
work of preaching and discipline. As the Heidelberg asserts, "The
kingdom of heaven is opened by proclaiming and publicly declaring to each and every believer that, as often as he accepts the gospel
promise in true faith, God, because of what Christ has done, truly
forgives his sins" (Q&A 84). Preaching, then, is a way that opens
and closes heaven. Furthermore, when churches fence the Lord's
Table they perform an act of discipline. Even the man who preaches
and administers the sacraments may do so only after he has passed

the scrutiny of the church's courts. So the mark of discipline is part of worship even though not obviously on display.

Together, the marks of the church constitute the true church. Which is why the Westminster Confession of Faith states that "unto this catholic visible church, Christ has given the ministry, oracles, and ordinances of God." In the same way that the marks of the church tell us how to find the true church, so also corporate worship helps us identify the church. Worship is essential to the church's identity. If our Reformed confessional standards are correct, the church cannot be seen or known apart from worship that is Reformed according to the Word of God because worship is comprised of the ordinances that God has given to his church.

Perfecting the Saints

Worship is not only something that marks the true church but also an activity that disciples God's people. As the Great Commission (Matt. 28:18–20) teaches, discipleship is not a one-time quick fix but rather a constant and gradual process that is to last either until death or Christ's return. And because worship is regular (it occurs every week), consists of the ministry of the Word (i.e., preaching and sacraments), and is the means that Christ gave to his church for discipling the nations, worship is crucial to the work of making disciples. Worship, then, not only consists of the marks of the institutional church, but is also at the heart of what it means to be a disciple of Christ.

Such an understanding of worship and its importance to the gathering and perfecting of the saints involves a different understanding of the Christian life than the one that prevails in contemporary Christianity. Of course, believers need to worship because God alone deserves all praise and glory. But Christians also need worship for their own edification and comfort. The church in this world is a pilgrim people, in complete dependence on God for protection and sustenance as they cross through this wilderness on their way to the promised land. Believers need the manna of eternal life that only the "ministry, oracles, and ordinances of God" provide. Here we need to remember how similar our circumstances are to those of the Israelites at the time when Moses sang praise to God for deliverance from the house of Egypt.

In 1 Corinthians the apostle Paul writes, "Now these things happened as examples for us, so that we would not crave evil things as [the Israelites in the wilderness] also craved" (10:6). In other words, the example of Israel's pilgrimage in the wilderness was written for the church. And in worship Christians must see themselves as the wilderness people of God. Just like the Israelites, we *have* been saved, and we enjoy *now* the benefits of salvation. But we have not reached our final destiny, the promised land, which is to be with Jesus Christ in glory, to live and worship in the heavenly Jerusalem. In a spiritual sense, then, we are just like the Israelites. We live in the "in-between times," what theologians describe as the "already/not yet," the age between Christ's ascension into glory and his second coming. Hebrews makes the connection between the Old Testament and New Testament church explicit. The Old Testament saints were "strangers and exiles on the earth" who "desire[d] a better country, that is, a heavenly one" (Heb. 11:13, 16). Christians, too, wait for the city which is to come. "For here we do not have a lasting city, but we are seeking the city which is to come" (Heb. 13:14). Similarly, when Peter calls the church God's chosen people, he also recognizes that New Testament believers live in a spiritual wilderness, by referring to them as "aliens and strangers" (1 Peter 2:9–11).

In this pilgrimage of being conformed to the image of Christ, believers find themselves in a condition like that of the Israelites. We are weak and frail, tempted and threatened by the hardships of the journey, and constantly tempted to give up. Here the account of the Exodus is again very instructive. What follows the narrative of the Israelites crossing the Red Sea (chap. 14) and Moses' song (chap. 15) are instructions for the provision of manna, including

the practice of Sabbath-keeping, reinstituted after centuries of neglect under slavery (chap. 16). Israel had to master these rules and
follow God's commandments precisely. The Lord expressed his
displeasure with those Israelites who violated the Sabbath by going
out to gather manna on the seventh day: "How long do you refuse
to keep My commandments and My instructions?" (Exod. 16:28).
Being an Israelite then would have been difficult; God's instructions were new and unusual to that generation. Those who failed
to prepare for the Sabbath would go hungry. They would also eventually grumble at Moses because the diet was monotonous. But
this was the pattern that God designed to sustain his people
throughout the wilderness. As the Bible records, "The sons of Israel
ate the manna forty years" (Exod. 16:35). Here, too, are lessons for
Christian piety and the practice of worship because the gathering
of the saints in worship is the means that God has established to
gather and perfect the church until united with her Lord in the
new heavens and new earth. Like the Israelites, we need to master the rules for worshiping him. Like the Israelites, we avoid worship or ignore God's instructions for worship at the peril of growth
in grace.

Understanding the Christian life as a pilgrimage and worship
as manna in the wilderness reminds us who live in an industrial
culture that our walk in faith and obedience is not mechanical.
Believers are not robots whose batteries are recharged by ambi-
tious church programs, devotional retreats, or spiritual awakenings. Rather, God has made us into new creatures who need regular sustenance. The means of grace, that is, "the ministry, oracles,
and ordinances of God," are the food he has provided to feed the
church.

This organic metaphor should instill more humility in our
understanding of the Christian life as well as greater gratitude for
the privileges we enjoy as God's sons and daughters when we gather
for worship. We are in warfare and constantly tempted to sin. The

hymn commonly attributed to John Calvin, "I Greet Thee, Who My Sure Redeemer Art," teaches this point well:

> Thou art the life by which alone we live,
> And all our substance and our strength receive;
> Comfort us by Thy faith and by Thy Power,
> Nor daunt our hearts when comes the trying hour.

The apostle Paul voiced these same sentiments when he defended his ministry in 2 Corinthians. The treasure of the gospel given to the church in earthen vessels (4:7) was in constant danger: "afflicted in every way, but not crushed; perplexed, but not despairing; persecuted, but not forsaken; struck down, but not destroyed" (4:8–9). The temptations of pilgrimage in the wilderness were very real to Paul. He knew he was wasting away. But through the grace of God he did not lose heart (4:16). Through the means of grace, in other words through his ministry—Word and sacrament—he could see and taste and hear the unseen things. The simple elements of words, water, bread, and wine were of eternal significance because they represented unseen things. And, according to Paul, the simple means produced "an eternal weight of glory far beyond all comparison" (4:17).

In many Christian circles today believers are tempted not to avail themselves of the "ministry, oracles, and ordinances of God." They sometimes think that lots of church activities and parachurch organizations will provide the sustenance God's people really need. But God has only promised to bless the ministry of the Word that constitutes Christian worship. Undoubtedly, many nonchurch activities may be beneficial. But God's promises are not attached to them in the same way that they are to elements of worship. In sum, the manna of worship both gathers and perfects God's people who are in the wilderness of this world. The oracles of God are essential to the health of God's pilgrim people.

Peculiar Worship

Manna in the wilderness was a peculiar experience for the Israelites. It was unlike anything in their Egyptian diet. At times they were given to grumbling, for it was less appetizing than Egyptian fare. So too ought we to see something strange about the spiritual diet God provides for us. To change the metaphor, some have compared worship to the process of mastering a foreign tongue. "We must learn Christianity," writes William Willimon, "even as we learn a foreign language."[1] Peter Leithart suggests that "worship is language class, where the Church is trained to speak Christian."[2] One learns a language by mastering difficult rules through repetition. We have no hope of speaking any language fluently if its conjugations and declensions change every week.

What is the proper grammar of worship? In their zeal to reform worship, the Reformers condemned both Roman Catholic sacerdotalists, who claimed an automatic dispensing of God's grace, and the Anabaptist radicals, who denied the need for ritual in worship at all. But ironically, if one observes the worship practices of our day in some Presbyterian and Reformed churches, one could conclude that, 400 years later, the Anabaptist theology of worship has prevailed. Many churches display a disregard for precise rules and regulations in worship. It is common for megachurches today to offer a variety of styles in worship. One church has six different flavors of worship, according to its bulletin (which reads more like a menu), from traditional, focusing on "participation through hymn singing," to "an exhilarating, come as you are service using contemporary music and practical messages." Saturday night offers "a relaxed atmosphere where you feel right at home," and one Sunday morning meeting serves "a contemporary service, using dynamic music, dramas and life-related messages."[3]

This church offers fare that is familiar to the world. It may satisfy more tastes, but it could also be the equivalent of a return to Israel's diet in Egypt. Designer worship like this appears to reject

God's wilderness commandments for his people, while dismissing the means whereby God has determined to nourish his people. It apparently sanctions a range of choices, enabling everyone to sing his or her own song, and to do what is right in his or her own eyes. It is manna without its humbling and disciplining effects (Deut. 8:3–5), and thus fails to provide sustenance and spiritual growth. The effect is to reinforce the worldly appetites of a consumer rather than shaping believers' habits heavenward, "gathering and perfecting" them in this life while preparing them for the next.

The church that properly worships will be peculiar to the world. Its ways will seem odd and irrelevant, and its language will sound strange. In a word, God's holy pilgrims will appear to be sectarians. This is because the church, saved by God in order to worship him, sees itself in light of God's purposes, not the world's expectations. God has elected us by his good pleasure, delivered us from the bondage of sin, and set us apart from the world, where, like the Israelites in exile, we are to sing the Lord's song in a foreign land (Ps. 137:4).

At the same time, as the church worships and serves the Lord in the wilderness of this present life, she does so with confidence, knowing that God has provided manna from heaven. And while marching to Zion the church also worships and serves the Lord with the confidence of exalting her God in the holy of holies as her chief joy, even though the world, like Israel's pagan neighbors, does not understand.

4

The Holy Day
of Worship

Q How is the Sabbath to be sanctified?

A The Sabbath is to be sanctified by a holy resting all that day, even from such worldly employments and recreations as are lawful on other days; and spending the whole time in the public and private exercises of God's worship, except so much as is to be taken up in works of necessity and mercy.

(Westminster Shorter Catechism, 60)

The Sabbath is the day Christians are to set apart for private and public acts of worship. We assume that Reformed and Presbyterians understand that they are to worship God on the Lord's Day, which is the Christian Sabbath. Our purpose here is not to establish the "when" of worship—Scripture and our confessions have settled that point. Instead our aim in this chapter is to examine the "how" of worship. That is to say, we want to see how a proper observation of the Sabbath informs the way we think about and practice worship.

Our point is that the neglect, and in some cases violation, of the Sabbath throughout American Protestantism is tied directly to confusion about worship. And this confusion is what makes much of the debate about posting the Ten Commandments on the walls of courthouses and public schools so ironic. A return to the Decalogue would not just stamp out lying, cheating, stealing, and illicit sex, but it would also alter the way many of us spend our Sundays. Understanding worship from the perspective of keeping the Sabbath holy, then, has much to teach us about how to assemble for worship.

The Rhythm of Worship

Why has Sabbath-keeping declined in American Protestantism? Why has a practice that enjoyed universal acceptance among American Protestants from roughly 1776 until 1960 virtually disappeared in the last half of the twentieth century? The explanation is usually attributed to the rise of leisure activities and professional sports, the changing character of work wrought by the

63

industrial revolution and technology, and the triumph of the automobile that brought weekend resorts within reach of the middle class. In sociological terms, what happened was secularization, especially a secularized view of work and rest (read: leisure).

All of this is true, but it is not the whole story. When American Protestants changed their observance of the Lord's Day, they also developed a peculiar form of spirituality, a particular understanding of how spiritual growth should take place. This form of piety is connected to the cultural context of religious disestablishment. Since the War for Independence, American churches have found themselves in a religious free market where the most successful competitors are those that offer the most attractive product to religious consumers. Without financial support from the state, churches have been forced to adopt market strategies to grow and develop.

How do religious freedom and the disestablishment of churches shape Christian piety? The answer can be found in much of the corporate life of contemporary evangelical churches, which consists of highly programmed activities conducted throughout the week for all ages and interest groups. Without such activities potential members may look for another church with the right mix of programs for mom, the kids, teens, and dad, as well as singles and seniors. With a "seven-days-a-week" church, Sunday worship can be reduced to just one more program, no better and no worse than other church activities.

Equally detrimental to Sabbath observance has been the widespread popularity of revivalism. Not only have churches used revivals as a means to convert the lost and gain new members, but revivals have become the chief means for determining genuine spirituality. These intense and earnest times of spiritual awakening have been used to distinguish the saved from the lost. They are times when believers reaffirm their faith and sense once again the saving power of God. In other words, revivals indicate when the Spirit of God is at work. This way of thinking about revivals has contributed to the notion that genuine piety and spiritual growth come through the quantifiable means of church programs and the intensity of religious experience. Mountaintop experiences are assumed to be necessary for spiritual growth, and consequently churches respond by offering activities that produce such experiences.

Compared to these high-octane experiences, the Sabbath seems boring. The Bible and Reformed confessions, however, describe very differently the spiritual disciplines essential for the Christian life. In Exodus, just as Moses was descending from Mount Sinai, God reiterated the Sabbath command in his parting instructions: "You shall surely observe My Sabbaths" (31:13). The Sabbath is a "perpetual covenant" for all generations (31:16). God's intention was to bless his people through the constant and conscientious observation of the day, week after week and year after year. Believers are sanctified through a lifetime of Sabbath observance. In other words, the Sabbath is designed to work slowly, quietly, seemingly imperceptively in reorienting believers' appetites heavenward. It is not a quick fix, nor is it necessarily a spiritual high. It is an "outward and ordinary" ordinance (WSC 88), part of the steady and healthy diet of the means of grace.

North American Protestants, we have noted, are generally not in sync with this rhythm. Attracted to the inward and extraordinary, they commonly suffer from spiritual bulimia, binging at big events, then purging, by absenting themselves from God's prescribed diet. The problem with the spirituality of mountaintop experiences is that no one can live on the mountain. We all have to return to our day jobs. When people leave the retreat or Bible camp, or even the midweek small group, they discover their life is still the same: jobs are unpleasant, marriages are shaky, sickness and disease afflict. In contrast, the Sabbath is supposed to be a discipline that provides an oasis in the desert for pilgrims, whose life is marked by suffering. Unlike the church activities that clutter the rest of the week, the Sabbath is when believers spiritually assemble on Mount Zion to meet with their God, to hear him speak, and to partake spiritually of their Savior's body and blood. As the writer to the Hebrews pointed out, ". . . you have come to Mount Zion and to the city of the living God, the heavenly Jerusalem, and to myriads of angels, to the general assembly and church of the firstborn who are enrolled in heaven, and to God, the Judge of all . . ." (12:22–23).

Moreover, the diligent practice of Sabbath-keeping helps Christians to learn what we referred to in the last chapter as the grammar of Christian worship. In worship, Christians are engaged in the act of learning the language of Zion. By observing the Sabbath and faithfully attending the means of grace, believers can learn this language over time, through the sure and steady means of repetition.

Sanctifying the Sabbath Day

The fourth commandment reads, "Remember the sabbath day, to keep it holy" (Exod. 20:8). The Sabbath, accordingly, is a holy day because God himself sanctified it by his holy resting on the seventh day of creation. "For in six days the LORD made the heavens and the earth, the sea and all that is in them, and rested on the seventh day" (Exod. 20:11). A theology of the Sabbath must underscore the uniqueness of this day. Only when we understand the holiness of the Sabbath day do we begin to appreciate the holiness of Christian worship. But the idea of a Sabbath day in the New Covenant is under attack, especially by theologians who assert that, with the coming of Christ, all of life is a "Sabbath rest." Some go so far as to conclude that there is no longer anything particularly unique about the Sabbath, nor binding about its observance.

The flaw of this argument is easily detected if we apply the same logic to our tithing to the Lord. We ought to view the Sabbath and our use of time in the same way that we regard the tithe and the stewardship of our money. To set apart a portion of our income for the work of the church is not to acknowledge that ten-percent of our possessions belong to God. Rather, it expresses our conviction that all that we possess is the Lord's. Still, God's comprehensive lordship over our possessions does not remove the obligation to give to him a portion specifically for the work of his church. In a similar way, even though all of our days are to be used in service to God, we are still commanded to set apart one day in seven for special worship and service. While we live all of life in God's presence and within his eyesight, only in worship on the Lord's Day do we enter into the holy of holies. For this reason Isaiah refers to the Sabbath as God's own "holy day" (Isa. 58:13).

Lest we think the Sabbath was merely an Old Testament ceremonial institution, the New Testament renders a similar estimate, especially with the term that is introduced to describe the Christian Sabbath: the "Lord's Day." For instance, John was "in the Spirit on the Lord's Day" when he wrote the Book of Revelation (Rev 1:10). This language is similar to the "Lord's Supper" (1 Cor. 11:20), and it means the same thing. Just as the latter is the supper that belongs to the Lord, so the former is the day that is set apart and belongs to the Lord. The Lord's Supper is a holy meal; it belongs to the Lord, who ordained it so that we might remember his work of redemption. We must not regard the Lord's Day as an ordinary day, any more than we would treat the Lord's Supper as a common meal. In the early church, the association between the Lord's Day and worship was clear. The people that belonged to the Lord gathered for worship on the day belonging to the Lord, the Christian Sabbath. In the New Covenant, as in the Old, this was the day for "holy convocations" (Lev. 23:2–3).

The Sabbath, Holiness, and Worship

How then does the idea of one day set apart inform our attitude toward worship? One way of answering this question is to deduce that if the Sabbath Day is separate and unique, so are the activities of that day. Because the Bible teaches that the Sabbath is holy, it follows that we are to understand worship as holy activity. Just as the Lord's Day is set apart from the rest of the week, so the acts of worship are hallowed, or set apart, from the rest of the activities of life.

As obvious as this conclusion may seem, it has come under considerable challenge in our day. We are losing a sense of holiness and therefore of the idea that worship is holy activity. This challenge comes from two directions.

First, there are many Christians, especially in the Reformed and Presbyterian world, who emphasize the comprehensiveness of the lordship of Christ. A Christian world-and-life view extends to all areas and walks of life. This teaching rightly affirms the goodness of creation and the legitimacy of all legal callings. One need not be a preacher or a missionary to honor God in his or her labors. Whoever is called to be a farmer or a baker can also glorify God. Furthermore, the worldly things that farmers and bakers produce are not somehow immoral or beneath Christians. They are good gifts from God, who pronounced his creation was good. To work in God's good creation is not to enter into a realm that is separate from religion's influence or God.

But neither does this work bring one into a *holy* realm. Here is where a Christian world-and-life view can lead Christians astray. Some Reformed theologians have suggested that to distinguish between the church and the world, or between what is holy and what is common, is to embrace a dualism that compromises a fully orbed Reformed world-and-life view. Such a distinction, the argument runs, denies the goodness of creation.

The second challenge to the idea that worship is a holy activity is directly related to the first. It comes mainly from advocates of contemporary worship who want to remove what they see as the stuffiness and formality of traditional services. Because life in all its diversity is for the purpose of glorifying and serving God, some contend, why not give expression to that diversity in worship? Why not encourage gifted artists and musicians to display their God-given talents in worship, through skits, special music, dance, and the like? To be sure, most advocates of contemporary worship find it necessary to draw some distinctions. John M. Frame, for example, writes, ". . . there are differences between what we have called the 'broad' and the 'narrow' senses of worship," but he goes on to write that "those differences are not always precisely definable."[1] And so when it comes to public worship on the Lord's Day, he denies that "there is a sharp distinction between what we do in the meeting and what we do outside of it. . . . All the earth is God's temple."[2]

It does not take much time to consider how this line of thinking may be abused. Frame continues:

> We must also make distinctions of this sort that are implicit, though not explicit, in Scripture. Scripture does not, for example, explicitly forbid juggling exhibitions at worship meetings. But Scripture does set forth the purposes of worship meetings; and entertainment—even though lawful at other times, is not *normally* consistent with those purposes. We may even say that entertainment, when it is consistent with biblical standards, is a form of "worship in the broad sense." But it is *generally* inconsistent with the purpose of a worship meeting.[3]

Notice what has happened to worship in this logic. The so-called Reformed world-and-life view—the notion that all of life is worship in a broad sense—quickly obscures biblical teaching about holiness. All that Frame can say about juggling is that it is not *normally* consistent with worship, that it is *generally* inconsistent with it. This leaves open the possibility that there may be particular times when juggling is appropriate because it is a form of worship in a broad sense. By this route all sorts of innovation (what John Calvin called frivolity) may find their way into worship.

In other words, the distinctions that are foundational to our observance of the Sabbath and our assembling for worship collapse in much contemporary writing that refrains from underscoring the biblical teaching on holiness. If we do not continue to stress the difference between the church and the world, as well as the difference between holy activities and times, and common work and times, we end up undermining the idea that in worship we assemble with all the saints and angels before the throne of God, a place that is none other than the holy of holies.

Later we will examine in some detail the specific activities that are appropriate in worship. But the concept of holiness furnishes a good starting point. For now we can say that only holy activities are appropriate because God has appointed them as the means for his holy people to glorify his name and to grow in grace. From this basis we can avoid much confusion about worship.

The Profane and the Common

Scripture insists that we connect holiness especially to Sabbath-keeping. The Sabbath Day is holy because it is that particular time when God's people give heightened corporate expression to their calling as saints, or holy ones. To understand the holiness of the Sabbath and worship, we must contrast it with biblical teaching on profanity. To be worldly in our observance of the Sabbath is to profane the day by treating it with contempt, desecrating and polluting that which God has set apart as holy. Through his prophet Ezekiel, God lays this charge upon Judah:

> Her priests have done violence to My law and have profaned My holy things; they have made no distinction between the holy and the profane, and they have not taught the difference between the unclean and the clean; and they hide their eyes from My sabbaths, and I am profaned among them. (Ezek. 22:26)

A similar example comes from Leviticus. Because Aaron's sons, Nadab and Abihu, offered strange fire and worshiped in a way that God had not commanded, he "consumed them, and they died before the LORD" (10:2). In this context God had instructed the priests of Israel "to make a distinction between the holy and the profane, and between the unclean and the clean" (10:10). Thus, the distinction between the holy and the profane lies at the heart of biblical teaching about the Sabbath and worship.

In these examples, the acts of profanity punished by God are things he has not commanded. So there is a clear commandment from Scripture for God's holy people not to profane the Sabbath by engaging in activities he has not prescribed. But there is more. The Reformed confessions in their teaching on the Lord's Day further distinguish among the holy, the profane, and the common or lawful. How is the Sabbath to be sanctified or kept holy? The Westminster Larger Catechism answers, "The Sabbath is to be sanctified by a holy resting all the day, not only from such works as are at all times sinful, but even from such worldly employments and recreations as are on other days lawful" (Q&A 117). The catechism is pointing out a third category for evaluating what is permissible on the Sabbath. There are things we do during the week that are legitimate and worthwhile. They are part of our vocation, like baking and farming. And there are recreations that are valuable and permissible, even such activities as juggling. But the catechism suggests that not only would juggling be impermissible in worship, but also it may not even be something we would do on the Lord's Day. Even though it may be lawful on ordinary days of the week, that is no guarantee that it is fit for the holy day.

Here another example from the Old Testament is helpful. In Jeremiah, God instructs his people, "You shall not bring a load out of your houses on the sabbath day nor do any work, but keep the sabbath day holy" (17:22). These common activities are certainly lawful during six days of the week, but they are forbidden on the day reserved for holy activities. Also in Nehemiah we see these lawful works expressly condemned as wicked and profane: "What is this evil thing you are doing, by profaning the sabbath day? Did not your fathers do the same, so that our God brought on us and on this city all this trouble? Yet you are adding to the wrath on Israel by profaning the sabbath" (Neh. 13:17–18). The prohibition against lawful and common activities on the Sabbath extends beyond work and includes even leisure pursuits that are lawful on other days. Only by turning away from our own pleasure do we call the Sabbath a delight and honor it as a holy day of the Lord (Isa. 58:13).

Some might accuse us of espousing a harmful dualism at this point. But such a charge misunderstands the biblical teaching on holiness. To mark the Sabbath as holy is not license for six days of secularization. We live all of life in the presence of God. But believers engage in activities during the week that are common to them and nonbelievers. Only believers, however, assemble on the holy day to participate in the holy activity of worshiping God. They come corporately to Zion, assemble before him who is the consuming fire, and meet Jesus at the mercy seat on the Lord's Day.

In another sense the charge of dualism is false because, strictly speaking, it doesn't go far enough. The biblical picture might be better described as trichotomous instead of dualist. Scripture instructs us to distinguish among activities that are holy, those that are inherently sinful, and those that are common or lawful on other days. These three categories are crucial both in sanctifying the Lord's Day and in understanding what is acceptable in worship. Unless these categories are preserved, the holiness of worship and the Sabbath will be distorted.

Recovering Holiness

God calls Christians to live holy lives. He calls us to live in the world and to work out our salvation in fear and trembling. He also commands us, at set times and places, to participate in holy things that are distinct from the ways of the world. God has given us a holy meal (the Lord's Supper), holy water (baptism), holy words (preaching), and a holy vocation (the minister of the Word). He has also given us holy time: one day for worship and rest. Contrary to popular claims, Reformed Christians do believe in a liturgical calendar. But it is weekly, not seasonal. Nor is it based on the programming of large congregational or parachurch ministries. Rather, it is the outward and ordinary cadence of Sabbath-keeping.

It is no coincidence, we believe, that a crisis in Reformed worship is taking place in an age of declining Sabbath observance. Skits that mimic television sitcoms and sermons that start with late-night television "top ten lists" are possible once Christians have forgotten about the holiness of the Sabbath. But by recovering the Sabbath as a holy day set apart for holy activities, the church has an opportunity to return to worship that is acceptable and pleasing to God. When we enter the holy of holies on the Lord's Day, we are engaged in practices that may only be "outward and ordinary." But they are also uncommon because they are holy.

Attention to the sanctification of the Sabbath and distinguishing between those practices that are legitimate and illegitimate ways of observing the day should also inform the way we worship. For crucial to keeping the Sabbath holy is observing the holy activities that comprise the worship of the only living and true God.

5

Acceptable Worship

Q What is the acceptable way of worshiping the only true God?

A The acceptable way of worshiping the true God is instituted by himself, and so limited by his own revealed will, that he may not be worshiped according to the imaginations and devices of men, . . . or any other way not prescribed in the Holy Scripture.

(Westminster Confession of Faith, 21.1)

How do we know that we have worshiped well? Is it a case of finding the Sunday morning service "meaningful" or "dynamic" or "exhilarating"? Or what about the visitors? Should the service be warm and accommodating to nonbelievers? Despite what the current literature on worship suggests, none of the criteria implicit in these questions establishes the acceptable way of worshiping God because they obscure the biblical standard for worship. Scripture insists that we must worship in a way that is acceptable to God. The simple test for good worship, then, is whether it conforms to the Bible. This standard has become known in Reformed churches as the *regulative principle*.

Reformed According to Scripture

The essence of the Protestant Reformation in the sixteenth century was the abandonment of medieval Catholic abuses and a return to the simplicity of Christian worship in the early church. The goal of all the Reformers was to be Reformed "according to the word of God." Submission to the rule of Scripture was the essence of the Reformation principle of Scripture's sufficiency. It is found, for example, in article 6 of the Thirty Nine Articles of the Church of England: "Holy Scripture containeth all things necessary to salvation; so that whatsoever is not read therein, nor may be proved thereby, is not to be required of any man, that it should be believed as an article of faith, or be thought requisite as necessary to salvation." Similarly, the Lutheran tradition, as articulated in the Augsburg Confession, condemns the Roman Catholic mass because "its traditions were preferred far above the commandments of God."

77

More specifically, the authority of Scripture in worship is a logical consequence of the Ten Commandments. This is, in fact, the place where the Reformed confessions and catechisms derive the doctrine of the regulative principle of worship. This teaching states that there are two ways of offering false worship. First, if one worships a false God, this is a violation of the first commandment. Second, if one worships the true God in a false way, this is a violation of the second commandment. Among the duties of the second commandment are "the receiving, observing, and keeping pure and entire, all such religious worship and ordinances as God hath instituted in his Word," including "the disapproving, detesting, [and] opposing all false worship" which are "monuments of idolatry" (WLC, Q&A 108).

To be Reformed in worship, however, requires going beyond the Lutheran and Anglican teaching and restricting the elements of worship only to what God has prescribed in his Word and nothing more. The Reformed saw other Protestants as inconsistent in their submission to the authority of Scripture. For Lutherans and Anglicans, the Bible was the sole authority for doctrine, but not for the government or the worship of the church. They affirmed in worship what has been called the "normative principle": whatever Scripture does not forbid is permissible. Thus, they bar from worship only what is specifically condemned in Scripture. So, for instance, because the Bible does not forbid burning incense, churches may use it in public worship.

For the Reformed, however, *sola Scriptura* means the reformation of doctrine, polity, and worship. All three are essential to the ministry of the church. Consequently, in applying the regulative principle to worship, the Reformed permitted only what God expressly prescribed in the Bible, believing that Scripture forbids in the church corporately identified whatever God does not command explicitly or by good and necessary consequence. In contrast to the normative principle, the *silence* of Scripture regarding a specific practice in worship, such as lighting candles or displaying banners, is just as much a prohibition as a direct condemnation of such a practice.

The regulative principle has important implications for some of the recent developments in American Protestant worship. Some Presbyterian congregations, for instance, have recently added dance and drama to their order of worship. However, Presbyterians who are self-consciously Reformed contend that there must be clear warrant in Scripture for these innovations. Moreover, if grounds can be found for adding dance and drama, then these activities should be required of all churches and are not merely optional. The only proper ground for doing anything in worship is a command from God in his Word.

Because of the regulative principle, simplicity has characterized Reformed worship. Without biblical warrant for many of the features of Roman liturgy, the Reformed tradition limited worship to the basics of the Word, sacraments, and prayer. Reformed Christians worship without candles, liturgical vestments, or highly ornamented sanctuaries. While Luther argued that God had given man five senses to use in worship, Calvin argued that we worship for God's glory, only secondarily for our edification, and not in the least for our pleasure. For this reason Calvin concluded about ceremonies of any kind in worship, "the more it delights human nature, the more it is to be suspected by believers."[1] In sum, the regulative principle simply states that whatever we do in worship must have support from the Bible. This is not to say that we have a prooftext for everything we do in worship. Scripture gives the church no exact order of worship. But by good and necessary consequence we may deduce from God's Word the necessary "parts of the ordinary religious worship of God" (WCF 21.5).

A Puritan Invention?

Critics of the regulative principle have argued that it was invented by the Puritans. The critics mean that this doctrine is peculiar to the Anglo-American Reformed tradition, that is, to Presbyterians who subscribe to the Westminster Standards, as opposed to the Reformed on the European continent, such as the Dutch, French, German, Hungarian, and Swiss churches. Accordingly, Presbyterians are overly concerned about a doctrine that has no counterpart among the descendants of the Reformed churches on the east side of the English channel.

A study of continental Reformed creeds and confessions, however, quickly exposes the error of this allegation. For example, the Heidelberg Catechism demonstrates that the regulative principle is the explicit consequence of the second commandment, which requires "that we in no wise make any image of God, nor worship him in any other way than he has commanded in his Word" (HC, Q&A 96). Similarly, the Belgic Confession states:

> In the meantime we believe, though it is useful and beneficial, that those who are rulers of the Church institute and establish certain ordinances among themselves for maintaining the body of the Church, yet that they ought studiously to take care that they do not depart from those things which Christ, our only Master, has instituted. And therefore we reject all human inventions, and all laws which man would introduce into the worship of God, thereby to bind and compel the conscience in any manner whatever. Therefore we admit only of that which tends to nourish and preserve concord and unity, and to keep all men in obedience to God. For this purpose, excommunication or church discipline is requisite, with all that pertains to it, according to the Word of God. (BC, art. 32)

When we look beyond the Reformed confessions, we also find evidence that John Calvin himself clearly espoused the regulative principle of worship. In *The Necessity of Reforming the Church*, he wrote:

I know how difficult it is to persuade the world that God disapproves of all modes of worship not expressly sanctioned by His Word. The opposite persuasion which cleaves to them, being seated, as it were in their very bones and marrow, is, that whatever they do has in itself a sufficient sanction, provided it exhibits some kind of zeal for the honour of God. But since God not only regards as fruitless, but also plainly abominates, whatever we undertake from zeal to his worship, if at variance with his command, what do we gain by a contrary course? The words of God are clear and distinct: "Obedience is better than sacrifice." "In vain do they worship me, teaching for doctrines the commandments of men" (1 Sam. 15:22; Matt. 15:9). Every addition to his word, especially in this matter, is a lie. Mere "will worship" (Col. 2:23) . . . is vanity. This is the decision, and when once the judge has decided, it is no longer time to debate.[2]

Consequently, if the regulative principle is so firmly established in the Reformed tradition, why are both Presbyterian and Reformed churches abandoning it? One objection unhappily gaining ascendancy in Reformed circles is that the regulative principle is a hyperscrupulous and narrow-minded rule that robs Christians of the freedom that God would have them express in worship. But ironically, as we shall see, the regulative principle is the surest guarantor of Christian freedom, not the notion that we may do whatever Scripture does not forbid.

Based on Reformed Doctrine

A common criticism of the regulative principle is that it is an Old Covenant idea. As such, it is illegitimate to import aspects of Israel's understanding of worship into the New Covenant, since the ceremonial law — including the Levitical restrictions on worship—has been fulfilled in Christ. Yet there is ample New Testament evidence for the regulative principle. In the quotation above from Calvin we find Jesus reiterating the prophet Isaiah's invocation of the regulative principle: "But in vain do they worship Me, teaching as doctrines the precepts of men" (Matt. 15:9; see Isa. 29:13). Calvin also cites Paul's condemnation in Colossians: "the commandments and teachings of men . . . are matters which have, to be sure, the appearance of wisdom in self-made religion and self-abasement and severe treatment of the body, but are of no value against fleshly indulgence" (Col. 2:22–23). On the basis of this passage, Calvin argued that the Bible prohibits "will worship," that is, worship that follows the man's will instead of God's as the rule of worship for the church.

Jesus further establishes the regulative principle in the Great Commission, in which he directs the ministry of the church "to observe all that I commanded you" (Matt. 28:20). There is no other authority for the church—including her worship—beside the teaching of Christ, who in his office as prophet reveals God's will for our salvation by his Word and his Spirit. To observe the Lord's authority is to worship as he has commanded. So the very charter for the New Testament church is expressed in the same terms of the law of Moses, namely, to exclude human invention from her teaching and worship.

The New Testament itself refutes the claim that the regulative principle is a ceremonial burden from which the church, having come of age in Christ, is now at liberty to worship as she sees fit. This principle cannot be abandoned by appealing to the discontinuities between the Old and New Covenants. Instead, the principle abides because it is premised on such unchanging truths as the character of God, the extent of human depravity, and the command to love our neighbor. These three truths all inform the New Covenant observance of the regulative principle.

It is obvious that the Bible reveals God to be a jealous God. His very name is "Jealous" (Exod. 34:14). This feature of his character is specifically revealed in the prohibitions against false worship. The Westminster Larger Catechism gives these reasons for the regulative principle from the second commandment: ". . . his fervent zeal for his own worship, and his revengeful indignation against all false worship, as being a spiritual whoredom" (Q&A 110). Because God is a jealous God, he does not welcome forms of worship that believing men and women may devise, even if they are well meaning and sincere. Instead, he insists that he be worshiped only as he commands (Exod. 34:13–15). Thus the Bible describes as wicked, irreverent, and profane not only those who contradict God's will, but also those who do what is beside his will.

The regulative principle also follows necessarily from Calvinism's doctrine of total depravity. Paul teaches in Romans that the entire human race is in rebellion against God. This rebellious spirit, of course, extends to worship and makes it false. Paul writes that the worship of unbelievers is false not because of ignorance but rather because of moral turpitude: "For even though they knew God, they did not honor Him as God. . . ." (1:21). Calvinists believe that depravity extends beyond the reprobate, and includes even the regenerate who still bear the corruption of sin. For this reason, those who are in Christ are incompetent to devise by their imaginations, even devout ones, any sort of worship that is appropriate or pleasing to God.

Consider, for instance, how the Westminster Confession describes good works. After we have done our duty toward God, we are still "unprofitable servants," and our good works are "defiled and mixed with so much weakness and imperfection" (16.5). What the confession says here of good works is certainly true of Christians' best efforts at worship. If we are incapable of doing good works untainted by corruption, how can we be able to devise worship that is pleasing to God solely on the basis of our own wisdom or desires?

Because of the doctrine of total depravity Calvin taught that the regulative principle is essential to true worship. All men possess the depraved inclination to suppress the truth and to worship idols. For that reason, Calvin concluded that "experience teaches us how fertile is the field of falsehood in the human mind, and that the smallest of grains, when sown there, will grow to yield an immense harvest." This idolatrous propensity remains strong even in believers, Calvin insisted, which is why he called the mind a "factory of idols," and wrote that "everyone of us is, even from his mother's womb, a master craftsman of idols."[3]

The Guardian of Christian Liberty

When we focus on the jealousy of God and the depravity of man, we have ample reason to be aware of the sinful impulses that still influence believers in worship. But restraint of sin is not to be confused with restraint of liberty. Contrary to the modern mindset that prizes unfettered freedom, the regulative principle is the very guardian, not the enemy, of Christian liberty in public worship. This follows from Paul's teaching on the conscience of weaker brothers (see Rom. 14 and 1 Cor. 8). Even if critics of the regulative principle are not convinced by inferences from God's jealousy and man's depravity, out of love for neighbor, they should, we believe, follow the regulative principle. As Paul teaches, they have an obligation not to wound the conscience of weaker brothers and sisters.

T. David Gordon has aptly applied this Pauline principle well to worship.[4] When the elders of the church call the people of God to worship, they are necessarily and unavoidably binding the conscience of worshipers (because Christians are forbidden to forsake the worship of God). This is not a problem if the church is worshiping biblically because the elders of the church are binding consciences according to the Word of God, as they are called to do in the Great Commission. But imagine a worship service that involves something without biblical warrant, such as the lighting of an advent wreath. If a believer finds this practice objectionable,

what can he or she do? Either one must not participate (which sinfully breaks a divine command to worship God with the rest of the
saints assembled) or one must participate (which sinfully violates
one's conscience).

Seen in this light, as Gordon tellingly argues, the regulative principle of worship, far from restricting Christian liberty, serves instead
to protect it. The only way in which a church can worship God
and protect liberty of conscience is to observe the regulative principle, that is, to worship as God has commanded. Properly
observed, it liberates worshipers from the tyranny of churches that
impose on their people elements of public worship that have no
biblical warrant. When churches engage in unbiblical practices
(whether for the sake of tradition or innovation), they usurp the
lordship of Christ, and automatically bind in an illegitimate fashion the consciences of believers. The sad and nearly inevitable
result is the outbreak of controversy and disharmony in the church.

Elements and Circumstances

Although the confessions of Reformed and Presbyterian churches
are explicit about the regulative principle, a moment's reflection
reveals that every consistory or session makes certain decisions about
worship that have no direct warrant from Scripture whatsoever. For
example, many churches have determined to call the people of
God to worship at 11 a.m. and 6 p.m. on the Lord's Day. Why not
10 a.m. and 7 p.m.? Or why not all day? It would not be unbiblical to worship from dawn to dusk. Moreover, churches have also
determined that the ministry of the Word is more effective with certain lighting, climate control, and voice amplification, and Scripture warrants none of this. And how do we determine how many
psalms and hymns to sing in worship? What is too few and what is
too many, and where do we find that in the Bible?

To answer these questions the Reformed and Presbyterian tradition offers another useful distinction, between the "elements" of

worship and its "circumstances." The elements of worship are the "what" of worship, the fixed and unchanging parts of the worship service. These include prayer, the reading and preaching of the Word, singing, and the sacraments.

The circumstances are the "how" of worship. These are the conditions that are most conducive to worship that is decent and orderly, including time and place. The Westminster Confession affirms this distinction when it states: ". . . there are some circumstances concerning the worship of God, and government of the church, common to human actions and societies, which are to be ordered by the light of nature, and Christian prudence, according to the general rules of the Word, which are always to be observed" (1.6). Thus, while there is no biblical reason not to worship from dawn to dusk on the Lord's Day, such observance would be imprudent, a "circumstance concerning the worship of God" that would put an onerous burden on believers.

More will be said about the elements and circumstances of worship in chapter 10. But for now the point is a simple one: far from loosening the strength of the regulative principle, this distinction between worship's elements (the "what") and circumstances (the "how") *clarifies* the regulative principle. The Bible tightly regulates what happens in public worship, while at same time allowing for variety in the circumstances that affect the way churches practice the elements of Reformed worship.

The Blessings of Reformed Worship

We must not forget that the second commandment reveals not only a God of wrath but also a God who is infinite in his mercy. The very passage that warned of a jealous God's judgment on false worship also promised God's "lovingkindness to thousands, to those who love Me and keep My commandments" (Exod. 20:6). Only the faithful observance of the regulative principle enables Christians to claim this promise. In his book *Worship That Is Reformed According to*

Scripture, Hughes Oliphant Old drew a conclusion about the differences between historic Reformed worship and recent innovations among American Protestants. He wrote that a program for renewing the church based on Word, sacraments, and prayer "may not be just exactly what everyone is looking for." Old continues:

> In our evangelistic zeal we are looking for programs that will attract people. We think we have put honey on the lip of the bitter cup of salvation. It is the story of the wedding of Cana all over again but with this difference. At the crucial moment when the wine failed, we took matters into our own hands and used those five stone jars to mix up a batch of Kool-Aid instead. It seemed like a good solution in terms of our American culture. Unfortunately, all too soon the guests discovered the fraud. Alas! What are we to do now? How can we possibly minister to those who thirst for the real thing? There is but one thing to do, as Mary the mother of Jesus, understood so very well. You remember how the story goes. After presenting the problem to Jesus, Mary turned to the servants and said to them, "Do whatever he tells you." The servants did just that and the water was turned to wine, wine rich and mellow beyond anything they had ever tasted before.[5]

The challenge Presbyterians and Reformed face today is precisely the one Mary faced. If we desire worship that is pleasing and acceptable to God, we must put aside "the imaginations and devices of men." In the words of the Heidelberg Catechism, "we should not be wiser than God" (Q&A 98). Instead, our purpose should be to worship God in a manner that is Reformed according to the Word of God. The regulative principle is nothing more and nothing less than the Reformed tradition's effort to do exactly that—worship God in a way pleasing to him on the basis of his revealed will in holy Scripture.

6

Reformed Liturgy

 What is the proper way to worship God with decency and order?

The way to worship with decency and order is to follow the pattern of God's covenant of grace: ". . . I will also have compassion on her who had not obtained compassion. And I will say to those who were not My people, 'You are My people!' And they will way, 'You are my God!'"

(Hosea 2:23)

How much are the current disputes about worship the result of an impoverished definition of worship? If all Presbyterians and Reformed could agree about what constitutes worship, wouldn't our services all be and look the same? Consider, then, the following definitions. "Worship," writes one theologian, "is the work of acknowledging the greatness of our covenant Lord."[1] According to another Reformed thinker, "Worship is the activity of the new life of a believer in which, recognizing the fullness of the Godhead as it is revealed in the person of Jesus Christ and His mighty redemptive acts, he seeks by the power of the Holy Spirit to render to the living God the glory, honor, and submission which are his due."[2] Still a third Reformed writer states that "true worship is that obedient service to God by the creature, submitting to God's will for how he will be thanked, praised, and remembered."[3]

All of these are good definitions. Each says something important about worship that can be supported from Scripture. But there is a dimension to worship that is omitted in all of them, and one that explains why good definitions of worship do not necessarily produce good or fitting services of worship. That dimension is the church, and more precisely the church as the gathering of God's people out of this world and into his presence. As we have argued, it is impossible to understand *public* worship apart from the church in its corporate or visible character.

When believers gather as a disciplined communion of saints, God is present among his people in a way different from his presence in our regular, daily lives. The church is the *ekklēsia*, called out of this world to honor and worship God, and to receive his mercy and blessing. While God is always and everywhere present among his people, his presence is special and unique in public worship on the Lord's Day. To come to worship is to meet him in the holy of holies. The *Directory for Worship of the Orthodox Presbyterian Church* puts it this way:

> A service of public worship is not merely a gathering of God's children with each other but before all else a meeting of the triune God with his people. God is present in public worship not only by virtue of the divine omniscience but, much more intimately, as the faithful covenant savior. The Lord Jesus Christ said, "where two or three are gathered together in my name, there am I in the midst of them."[4]

Of course, this gathering between God and his people is not a meeting among equals. For this reason we must regard worship as a *solemn assembly* and be very careful about how we conduct ourselves before God. Ecclesiastes warns against coming before God in a hasty or impulsive manner. When we do so we "offer the sacrifice of fools" who "do not know they are doing evil" (5:1–2).

What worshipers do during this solemn assembly is frequently called a "liturgy." That may seem like a dirty word among Reformed Christians, suggesting the Roman Catholic mass or the Episcopalian prayer book, accompanied by vestments, candles, and altars. Presbyterians, by contrast, are more at home in low church worship with freer and more open forms of worship that may be described as nonliturgical. But liturgy is not a word that Reformed and Presbyterian folk need fear. Here is how the Christian Reformed Church used it in its 1968 report on worship:

> Liturgy is what people do when they worship. . . . Every church has a liturgy, whether it worships with set forms inherited from the ages or whether it worships in the freedom of the moment. The only question is whether we have

the best possible liturgy: it is never whether we have a liturgy.[5]

The Covenant of Grace

What is *good* liturgy? A good liturgy follows an appropriate pattern and is suitable for the occasion. In particular, it is a fitting practice or embodiment of our theology. Bad liturgy, on the other hand, is a failure properly to act out our faith in forms suitable to the doctrines that we profess.

What then is good *Reformed* liturgy? It is liturgy that orders worship in a way that fits with Reformed doctrine. For this reason Presbyterians and Reformed should not expect to worship like charismatics or Anglicans. We believe that both are mistaken in their theology and worship, but at least they deserve credit for shaping their worship in ways that are appropriate to their theological convictions. Least of all should we worship in a way that suggests that our theology doesn't matter. The premises of Reformed theology — God's sovereignty, creation, and providence; man's depravity; Christ's mediation; the Holy Spirit's saving application of Christ's work; and the centrality of Scripture — should all be implicitly present in Reformed liturgy.

What gives Reformed worship its particular shape and direction is the same principle that forms the organizing principle of Reformed theology. No less than our theology, our worship must be arranged according to the doctrine of the covenant. The heart of our covenantal relationship with God is found in God's promise to Abraham: "I will establish My covenant between Me and you and your descendants after you throughout their generations for an everlasting covenant, to be God to you and to your descendants after you" (Gen. 17:7).

God's promise to Abraham is restated throughout the subsequent unfolding of God's covenant promises in redemptive history. These words are found in Jeremiah as God describes through his prophet the essence of the new covenant in Christ: "I will put My law within them and on their heart I will write it; and I will be their God, and they shall be My people" (Jer. 31:33). The prophecy of Ezekiel repeats this promise: "I will make a covenant of peace with them; it will be an everlasting covenant with them. And I will place them and multiply them, and will set My sanctuary in their midst forever. My dwelling place also will be with them; and I will be their God, and they will be My people" (Ezek. 37:26–27).

Paul cites these prophecies to show their fulfillment in the new covenant. "For we are the temple of the living God; just as God said, 'I will dwell in them and walk among them; and I will be their God, and they shall be My people" (2 Cor. 6:16). Likewise, the author of the epistle to the Hebrews links the work of Christ, the mediator of a better covenant, to the covenant God originally established with Abraham and his descendants: "For this is the covenant I will make with the house of Israel after those days, says the LORD: I will put My laws into their minds, and I will write them on their hearts. And I will be their God, and they shall be My people" (Heb. 8:10). The book of Revelation describes the ultimate fulfillment of this promise in the marriage of Jesus and his bride, the church in the new heaven and new earth: "Behold, the tabernacle of God is among men, and He will dwell among them, and they shall be His people, and God Himself will be among them. ..." (21:3).

These texts form the basis for the way we should structure our public worship. God is our God and we are his people. God promises, and his people respond to his mercy in obedience and consecration. God acts in redemption, and we respond in gratitude and service. God speaks to us, and we respond in praise. Following this pattern, Christian worship is inherently covenantal. Recall the words above from the OPC's *Directory for Worship*: "God is present in worship not only by virtue of the divine omniscience, but, much more intimately, as the faithful savior."[6] Because God is our God and redeemer, corporate worship involves a sacred dimension where the church gathers in the very holy of holies. The church's assembling for worship, then, should be a re-enactment of the covenantal relationship between God and his people.

The Dialogical Principle

The covenantal pattern of Christian worship takes the shape of a dialogue between God and his people. The *Directory for Worship of the Orthodox Presbyterian Church* describes the dialogue in this way:

> The parts of worship are of two kinds: those which are performed on behalf of God, and those which are performed by the congregation. In the former the worshipers are receptive, in the latter they are active. It is reasonable that these two elements be made to alternate as far as possible.[7]

Furthermore, this principle of a dialogue is found throughout biblical demonstrations of worship. According to Genesis, to be in covenant with God is "to call upon the name of the LORD" (Gen. 4:26). To call upon God's name and to invoke his presence require bowing down and worshiping him, in reverence, humility, and submission. After the flood Noah dialogued with God through a burnt offering that rose to heaven, with smoke that filled God's nostrils with a pleasing aroma (Gen. 8:20–21). When meeting God on Mount Sinai, Moses "made haste to bow low toward the earth and worship" (Exod. 34:8). Similarly, when witnessing the risen Christ, John "fell at His feet like a dead man" (Rev. 1:17).

To be sure, these were terror-provoking encounters. For instance, the prophet Isaiah was overwhelmed with despair over his sinfulness when he confronted the true and living God: "Woe is me, for I am ruined! Because I am a man of unclean lips, and I live among a people of unclean lips; for my eyes have seen the King, the LORD of hosts." (Isa. 6:5). Coming into the presence of the God who established the covenant of grace involves terror and comfort, since that covenant reveals both his infinite righteousness and mercy. Still, the Israelites exhibited confidence when they sought God in the way in which he prescribed. After retaking the oaths of the covenant during the reforms of King Asa, the kingdom of Judah rejoiced, ". . . for they had sworn with their whole heart and had sought Him earnestly, and He let them find Him. . . ." (2 Chron. 15:15). Likewise, the psalmist rejoiced that in covenantal dialogue with his God he could gain the assurance that his sins were forgiven (Ps. 32:1–5).

Several recent studies on worship have challenged the dialogical principle by suggesting that worship should have both "horizontal" and "vertical" aspects. The notion here is that in the vertical aspects we do things that honor and revere God, and in the horizontal dimension we edify the people. So good worship, some maintain, should contain both of these features, blending the vertical "godward" elements with the horizontal "edifying" elements.

But the principle of covenantal or dialogical worship, following biblical patterns of worship, challenges this distinction by insisting that all of worship is vertical. It is a holy transaction or conversation between God and his people. It is not a conversation among God's people. When we greet our neighbors in the next pew or when we listen to testimonies, we are not worshiping God. As edifying as these activities may be, and as encouraging as they are in the appropriate setting, corporate worship is a time when the dialogue goes back and forth between God and his people. It is a time—and one of the rare times during our busy weeks—when we need to hear that God is faithful and continues to be our God, and when we reaffirm our vows to be his faithful people.

This is not to suggest, however, that good liturgy doesn't bless the worshipers. Worship that is true certainly does edify. But it is precisely in the vertical character of worship that we receive our blessing, and we need not enhance it by adding a horizontal dimension to our liturgy. In meeting us for worship, God blesses us in several ways. At the beginning, the call to worship is our assurance that God is present among us. We have his words of forgiveness following our confession of sin. He speaks his word of instruction as the Word of God is read and preached. Finally, at the close of worship God blesses us with the words of benediction. The Westminster Shorter Catechism identifies the blessings inherent in vertically directed worship when it says of the Word read and preached that it becomes, by the work of the Spirit, "an effectual means of convincing and converting sinners, and of building them up in holiness and comfort, through faith, unto salvation" (Q&A 89).

The blessing of vertical worship is sufficient for our edification. We do not need to hear things from each other in worship to be blessed or encouraged or convicted. The best edification God's people can experience is to hear that the living and true God is our God and that he will have mercy on us and cause his face to shine upon us. We need not tinker with the dialogical structure to add therapeutic features that appear to give encouragement and support. The means of grace are sufficient to provide genuine hope and comfort because God has ordained them as the ways in which he will bless and sustain his people. We are not wiser than God, so we need to learn to take encouragement from those elements of worship that please him, rather than devising strategies that we think will be consoling. Just as the Israelites needed to be content with the food that God gave them during their wilderness pilgrimage, so we need to be content with the food from on high that sustains our spiritual lives.

The Gospel Logic of Worship

Having said that covenant theology involves a certain pattern in worship, we must also recognize, as the Reformed tradition has historically, that Scripture does not provide a fixed order of worship. Why don't we begin worship with the benediction or the offering? Why don't we place the sermon at the very end of worship, as the last thing we hear before we leave? It is not possible to find a clinching prooftext for answers to these questions. Yet, good reasons exist for avoiding such novelties. The covenantal structure not only establishes the dialogue between God and his people in the sacred and solemn assembly of worship, but also gives us assistance for the order of Reformed worship. As Terry Johnson has argued, covenant theology provides the "gospel logic" that undergirds public worship. In Johnson's words, this logic consists of four cycles of worship: praise, confession, the means of grace, and blessing.[8]

For instance, the Psalms instruct us to "enter . . . his courts with praise" (Ps. 100:4). Praise, according to Hughes Oliphant Old, is in fact the "gateway into God's presence." And so Reformed liturgy has historically begun by focusing the hearts of worshipers on praise, with elements such as:

    Call to Worship
    Invocation and Prayer of Praise
    Psalm or Hymn of Praise
    Confession of Faith
    Gloria Patri or Doxology

Again, even though the New Testament does not say, "when you gather for worship, be sure to start with a time of praise," praise is a fitting way to begin. Aside from being what God alone deserves, praise reinforces the reason Christians have assembled. The point of worship is to give God the glory for all that he has done.

Having begun worship with this vision of God and his glory, it is fitting that worshipers should be struck with a sense both of their finiteness and their unworthiness. In other words, after having considered God's greatness, we naturally become aware of our own sinfulness and the incongruity of sinners communing with a holy God in the holy of holies. This sense of seriousness and contrition should lead to a "cycle of confession" with the following elements:

Reading of the Law
Confession of Sin
Assurance of Pardon
Psalm or Hymn of Thanksgiving

One of the more striking phenomena of contemporary Reformed worship is how little time is given to a corporate confession of sin. Even more pointed is the growing uncomfortableness with the minister giving an assurance of pardon. Part of this may be a proper opposition to sacerdotalism. But however forgiveness of sins is declared in the service, it has to rank as one of the all-time riddles in the Reformed tradition that churches adhering to that theology have dispensed with a time of the service dedicated to the confession of sin and granting forgiveness. It is even more remarkable since Christ himself told his apostles that declaring forgiveness of sins would be their chief task: "If you forgive the sins of any, their sins have been forgiven them; if you retain the sins of any, they have been retained" (John 20:23).

Then after having contemplated God in his glory, seen ourselves in our own unworthiness, and been reminded of the forgiveness we have through Christ, we next need to grow in faith. And so a service may plausibly move into a cycle of worship that employs the means of grace:

Prayer of Illumination
Reading of Scripture
Sermon
Prayer of Intercession
Lord's Supper

In this part of the service, believers, like Mary (Luke 10:38–42), come to sit at the feet of Jesus and hear his instruction from the Word preached. In response, believers offer up petitions for their needs in the light of what has been preached. And finally, further nurture and comfort comes through the administration of the Supper in which, as the Westminster Shorter Catechism says, worthy receivers partake, "not after a corporal or carnal manner, but by faith" of Christ's body and blood "to their spiritual nourishment and growth in grace" (Q&A 96).

In the last part of the service, after having been built up in the faith, God's people respond with thanksgiving to God for his grace and mercy. In this final cycle of worship, the congregation engages in acts of thanksgiving and blessing:

Prayer for Offering
Collection
Concluding Hymn
Benediction

In other words, worshipers leave in a posture fitting the shape of the rest of their week. They depart from worship with gratitude on their lips, expressing willingness to serve God in the vocations he has given to them. At the same time, God has the last word in worship when the minister pronounces the benediction and once again, believers hear the good news of God's favor upon them in Christ.

With some variation, this is the structure of the liturgy that has characterized Reformed worship since John Calvin. Its guilt-grace-gratitude structure is patterned after the gospel that the Reformed faith has so consistently and adamantly sought to propagate and defend. As Terry Johnson concludes, worship in this way "is consistent with scriptural example, with Christian experience, and the Reformed tradition."[9]

Worship: Who Does What?

Much of the debate in worship today seems to have less to do with *what* comprises right worship than with *who* should be participating in worship. Who may pray in worship? Who should sing? Who should and should not preach? When are we active and when are we receptive?

In addressing these and similar questions, we are off to a good start if we begin with the dialogical principle of worship. Which part of the liturgical dialogue is represented in these acts of worship? Who is addressing whom? When is God speaking and who speaks for God? When are the people responding, and who speaks for the people of God? The dialogical principle forbids us from making distinctions in worship merely according to sex (only men can do certain things), or age (with sermons for the children or dismissing them to children's church), or musical gifts (with choirs and soloists who "minister" to the people in song). Instead, the dialogical principle instructs us to see worship as a meeting of two parties: God and his people.

As we argue in the following chapter in greater detail, the duties of worship should be divided in two. The special office of the minister of the Word speaks for God, and for the congregation in pastoral prayer. The general office of believers responds to God with song, confession, and praise. In these corporate responses to God, the people speak and sing with one voice, whether through the prayers of the pastor, songs sung from the hymnal, or creeds or prayers recited. Individual expressions are not in keeping with the corporate character of public worship. The distinction we are drawing here is not an argument for women's ordination. We believe that the Bible restricts the special offices of the church to men. But the key distinction in worship is not gender but ordination. And so the limitations on worship that Scripture extends to women apply equally to unordained men (unless those men are training for office).

It is imperative for Reformed Christians to restore the word *liturgy* to their theological vocabulary. To low-church Reformed and Presbyterians, the word may connote formalism and vain repetition. But as we have argued, another way to understand it is simply as a way of conducting the solemn assembly between God and his people. It establishes the pattern of the covenantal dialogue between God and his people: God speaks, and then we respond. God speaks again, and then we respond; and so on.

Reformed liturgy, then, is a blessed thing. Embodying the doctrine of the covenant of grace, it provides order and coherence in worship through a dialogical structure. Just as we have seen in the notion of the regulative principle, we must not try to be wiser than God. If we disregard the dialogical principle, if we become too lopsided with what we say instead of coming into his presence to hear him speak to us and then responding on the basis of what he has said and done, we will not only rob God of the adoration that is his due, but also deprive ourselves of the blessing he would have for us as he condescends to meet us.

7

Leading and Participating in Worship

Q How does church government shape the elements of worship?

A We believe that this true Church must be governed by the spiritual policy which our Lord has taught us in His Word—namely, that there must be ministers or pastors to preach the Word of God, and to administer the sacraments. . . . By these means everything will be carried on in the Church with good order and decency, when faithful men are chosen, according to the rule prescribed by St. Paul in his epistle to Timothy.

(Belgic Confession, art. 30)

The Westminster Larger Catechism contains some apparently perplexing teachings regarding the way that ministers and the laity participate in the worship service. For instance, question 156 asks, "Is the word of God to be read by all?" The answer is as follows: "Although all are not to be permitted to read the word publicly to the congregation, yet all sorts of people are bound to read it apart by themselves, and with their families. . . ." A few questions later (158), the divines ask a related query: "By whom is the word of God to be preached?" The answer is that "only . . . such as are sufficiently gifted, and also duly approved and called to that office" may preach. The latter of these questions is not particularly unusual since it is a rare thing for a Presbyterian or Reformed believer to advocate the rights of the laity to preach. When it comes to the sermon we expect ministers to assume their appointed place in the church building and the order of service. But what about the rest of the service? Is the Larger Catechism correct when it says that the laity may not read the Word publicly in worship? And by implication, does this mean that lay persons may not lead in worship at all? Are ministers the only ones allowed to be up front reading the Word, leading in prayer, preaching, and administering the sacraments? These are questions that some 350 years after the Westminster Assembly would not be as readily or unanimously answered by ministers or church members in Reformed communions.

A major reason for current retreat from what some might call the clericalism of the Westminster divines is the popular doctrine of the priesthood of all believers. Many American Protestants, Presbyterian and Reformed included, believe that the Reformation did away with any notion of superiority or hierarchy within the church. Clergy and laity are equal. Neither is somehow more sacred or spiritual. And this is because all Christians have direct access to God through Christ, the High Priest who sits at God the Father's right hand. Unlike the Old Testament tabernacle where only the high priest could enter the holy of holies, Christ's mediatorial work has abolished the restrictions of the old covenant and now all believers have access to the mercy seat. The implication of Christ's work for worship, according to some, is that our services in the new covenant should reflect the equal access to God's throne that all believers have by virtue of Christ's work. In other words, laity should be able to participate in worship by reading the Word, leading in prayer and song, or giving an occasional testimony of God's gracious provision.

Such an understanding of the priesthood of all believers and its application for worship, however, is more a function of North American conventions than an accurate reflection of Reformed teaching. As much as the Protestant Reformers taught the priesthood of all believers, they also believed that ministers were responsible for leading worship; laity should not because they had not been called to perform this service. For them, the priesthood of all believers did not apply to worship. Instead, it was a teaching that had a primary bearing on everyday life. All believers, no matter what their calling, whether pastor or carpenter, were priests in God's sight, and through the work God called them to do. Christians, whether ordained or not, were offering spiritual sacrifices to God by seeking his glory in their labors. The priesthood of all believers, then, gives every legitimate calling religious significance by teaching that all forms of work are valuable in God's sight and useful to his providential and redemptive plan. But the doctrine had very little to say about worship. For that reason, some attention needs to be given to the questions surrounding who leads and how Christians participate in worship.

Who Leads in Worship?

Reformed liturgy is based upon the covenantal character of the Christian religion. Throughout the history of redemption, God initiates in creation and redemption, and his creatures or people respond in acts of faith and obedience. The same pattern is seen in worship. God speaks by calling us into his presence in the invocation, through the reading and preaching of the Word, through the sacramental words of baptism and the Lord's Supper, and his covenant people respond in prayer, songs of praise, and affirmation of faith. This is the dialogical principle of Reformed worship. It underscores the fundamentally conversational character of the corporate assembly of the saints for worship. They gather to hear God speak, and they respond with speech which God himself governs in his revealed Word.

The dialogical principle of worship is a useful guide for figuring out who does what in worship, and especially who leads or officiates the service. As the Westminster Standards indicate, the Presbyterians and Puritans who gathered during the 1640s had a definite view that ministers and elders are solely responsible for leading worship. This is why the Larger Catechism teaches that the laity may not read the Bible in public worship. It also explains why the divines taught that only ministers could preach the Word. The same pattern held for the other elements of worship. Ministers gave the corporate prayers, administered the sacraments, pronounced the benediction. In other words, the person most visible in worship was the man behind the pulpit, the Lord's Table, or next to the font—the minister of the Word. Here is how a Christian Reformed Church member put it, recalling the status of Reformed ministers during the 1920s:

These older ministers, whose spiritual authority was enormous and sometimes tyrannical, had fixed minds. Their influence is sometimes hard to understand now when every

Tom, Dick, and Sadie with a strong D average in high school has the right to expressed opinion. Then, when preachers said, "Thus saith the Lord," they were inclined to believe it.[1]

This pattern governed American Presbyterian and Reformed worship until only recently. Prior to the 1960s worshipers would have seen ministers leading worship. Most believers understood, even if their minister was not tyrannical, that the pastor's duty was to preside over the worship service, and they readily acceded to it. But since the 1960s a democratic and expressive outlook has prompted questions about whether ministers leading worship is really a form of clerical dominance. Meanwhile, a number of popular works have argued for the idea of "every member ministry." For instance, Rick Warren, the pastor of the famous Saddleback Church, in his book *The Purpose Driven Church*, states that "every believer is a minister." He goes on to say that not every member is a pastor. But for Warren the main difference between the pastoral staff and church members is that the former perform the administrative duties while the latter do the real work of ministry, which is chiefly evangelism.[2]

Such an understanding of ministers and laity has obvious implications for worship. One is that worship becomes chiefly a time for outreach and evangelism. Worship committees design services to reach the unchurched so that growth in numbers replaces the spiritual growth of believers as the goal of worship. At the same time, the idea that all members are called to evangelize sets up a predicament for the tasks that clergy and laity perform during a service. If members are called to preach the gospel throughout the course of their lives, why is it that the pastor is the only one allowed to speak on Sunday? Some churches circumvent this dilemma by maintaining the practice of the pastor giving the sermon while the time is set aside for testimonies from lay members. Or even more popular is the use of worship leaders, that is, people from the congregation who lead in song (and while announcing the music will also introduce the songs and give instruction about the significance of the words or this part of the service). In sum, the reorientation of worship over the last thirty years has been most noticeable in greater participation by the laity in parts of the service reserved previously for the minister. And the rationale for this change has been the application of the idea of the priesthood of all believers; clergy are no longer as special as they used to be, and church members have risen to new levels of responsibility.

The funny thing about this transformation of church ministry is that few proponents of every-member ministry would think of applying this logic to other aspects of their lives. For instance, would anyone seriously want all those holding a savings account in a particular bank to run its investment portfolios? Or when it comes time for a tonsillectomy for a son or daughter, would the mother actually like to take the scalpel into her own hands? And the examples of expertise need not be limited to the world of professions. How many automobile owners would take their vehicle to a repair shop in which dentists and bakers performed the tune-ups and replaced the timing belts? The obvious answer is that today's Christians tolerate a high degree of hierarchical expertise when it comes to any number of society's functions, but refuse to do so when it comes to religious matters. We believe this is a mistake and represents a fundamental misunderstanding of the nature of office and ordination. The reasons for defending the rights of clergy to officiate public worship may differ from those upholding the expertise of realtors or lawyers, but that difference in no way weakens the specific work that pastors are called to do as ministers of Word and sacrament.

What Is Ordination For?

The form for ordination in both the Orthodox Presbyterian Church and the Christian Reformed Church says that the Bible

clearly teaches that the office of minister was instituted by the Lord
Jesus Christ himself. It was Christ's intent to build his body, the
church, through the ministry of the Word. The standard prooftext
for this teaching is Ephesians 4:12, where the apostle Paul establishes that Christ "gave some to be apostles; and some, prophets;
and some, evangelists; and some, pastors and teachers; for the perfecting of the saints, unto the work of ministering, unto the building up of the body of Christ" (ASV). This verse is crucial for understanding both the work for which ministers are ordained and recent
changes among conservative Protestants in their estimation of pastors. To be sure, lots more can be said about the meaning of this
verse, especially concerning its teaching about the relation among
the extraordinary offices of apostles and prophets and the ordinary
ones of evangelist, pastor, and teacher. But for now, since we are
looking exclusively at the work of ministers, our comments will be
limited to what this verse teaches about pastors.

The debates about the meaning of this verse concern how the
sentence should be punctuated. Older versions of the New Testament insert a comma between the phrases "for the perfecting of
the saints" and "unto the work of ministering." Contemporary trans-
lations, however, exclude that comma. And that comma says a lot
about what the work of ministers is. In the older versions, the work
of the pastor extended to the last three phrases of the verse. Accordingly, Christ gave his church pastors to perfect the saints, to minister, and to build the church. In other words, the pastor is an
undershepherd who nurtures the flock that Christ has entrusted
to him. Ministers have a special function, which is to minister to
God's people. This does not necessarily involve expertise or authority, but it does give the minister a different status from the rest of
God's people, which is care for the body of Christ through the
ministry of Word and sacrament, just as Christians in their various
vocations are called as parents to care for their children, farmers
to be good stewards of their land, and shopkeepers to be fair and
honest in their service to customers.

The other way of rendering Ephesians 4:12, the one without the comma, renders the work of the minister to be less important. According to this interpretation, pastors "perfect" believers so that they can perform the work of "ministering" to each other. In effect, what pastors do in this view is equip all Christians for the common work of building up all of the church. In other words, this is an every-member-ministry construction of Pauline teaching that diminishes the specialness of pastors' duties by elevating to the status of ministry all the service of encouragement and edification that believers quite appropriately offer to each other. The words of consolation spoken by a husband to his grieving wife, accordingly, become virtually the equivalent of the minister's preaching of the Word or pronouncing the benediction. To be sure, the husband may need to sit under the pastor's preaching for a while before being able to comfort his wife. But in the end, the removal of the comma in Ephesians 4:12 has the effect of eliminating the differences between the holy activities pastors are called to perform and the common (though nevertheless good) ones husbands extend to their families.[3]

These different readings of this verse from Paul's epistle to Ephesus help to make the point that notions of office and ordination can never be severed from function. Too often when the idea of special office comes up, many believers typically think of the men who rule in the church, the ones who have authority to make decisions, establish the budget, and discipline wrongdoers. Although the work of ministers and elders involves some of these duties, the idea of special office in terms of power and government obscures the pastoral dimension of church officers. For instance, the marks of the church in the classic Reformed articulation are preaching, sacraments, and discipline. All of these activities, which those ordained to the special offices of minister and elder perform, have been ordained by Christ to establish and feed his people until his return. This is not to say that the love ordinary believers show to each other is inconsequential. But in the case of the minister, the work of preaching the Word and administering the sacraments has a special importance because God has promised to bless these holy tasks to the end of establishing the body of his only begotten Son.

If the ordination of ministers sets them apart for holy activities rather than merely giving them the authority to moderate session or consistory meetings, the responsibilities ministers carry out says a lot about the nature of ordination and office. As stated above, holiness in the Bible has two senses, one having to do with setting apart for sacred purposes, the other having to do with personal qualities that flow from sanctification. Ordination falls into the prior sense — the church ordains men to carry out sacred work, namely, the preaching of the Word, administration of the sacraments, and the discharge of discipline. Ordination and office can never be isolated from function. The nature of pastoral work specifies the purpose of ordination and defines the official capacities of the officer. Of course, preaching, the sacraments, and discipline all imply authority. Not every member of the church has a commission to perform these functions. But the authority of these activities stems from Christ, the one who gave this work to his undershepherds.

Consequently, questions about who leads in worship are fairly easy to answer. The one who officiates in public worship is the church officer commissioned to do the work Christ gave to his disciples, namely, teaching (Word) and baptism (sacrament). To be sure, the worship service consists of more than Word and sacrament. As Calvin taught, it also includes prayer, which is proper rubric for considering congregational song. But with the exception of singing and confession of faith, the elements of worship all involve the work of the minister. He invokes God's presence by reading Scripture, prays on behalf of his flock, reads and preaches the Word, administers the sacraments, and pronounces the benediction. All of these activities are given to ministers. They are in the vocation of Word, sacrament, and prayer. So it comes as little surprise that the Westminster divines restricted not only the preaching of the Word but also its reading to pastors.

Worship: Active or Passive?

With the minister doing most of the work in the worship service, many might assume that little remains for the congregation but to sit and watch. In fact, one claim often made on behalf of contemporary worship is that it is much more participatory since it involves the people in the pews in forms of worship that encourage active engagement. Here a word needs to be said about how demandingly active the so-called traditional forms of worship are for the laity. The minister may be the one doing the speaking, reading, and praying, but such worship also requires believers to be ever alert and participating.

For instance, here is the instruction the Westminster Shorter Catechism gives on how to listen to a sermon. In order for the Word (preached and read) to be effective, answer 90 reads, "we must attend thereunto with diligence, preparation, and prayer, receive it with faith and love, lay it up in our hearts, and practice it in our lives." Of course, not all of this work on the part of those who hear the Word can be done while sitting in church. Some of it must take place in preparation for the observance of the Lord's Day, and some of it carries over into the workweek as believers seek to heed God's Word in their vocations. But plenty remains to be done during the service, such as hearing the Word diligently and prayerfully, and receiving it with faith and love. Worshipers are not inactive. Listening and appropriating are activities that require concentration and spiritual discipline. And this is partly what Christ was trying to teach Martha in Luke 10:38–42. When it comes time to be in the Lord's presence as we are in worship and to hear his undershepherd expound the Word, as Christ told Martha who was busily occupied with entertaining, "only one thing is necessary" (10:41). And that one thing was what Mary had chosen, which was to sit at Jesus' feet and listen to his Word. So even in the most apparently passive of activities, such as listening to a sermon, so-called traditional worship requires active partici-pation from those who would believe and do the Word.

The same can be said for the sacraments. According to the West-minster Standards, receiving the Lord's Supper takes a lot more endeavor than simply eating a piece of bread and drinking a small portion of wine. "It is required of them," reads the Larger Cate-chism, that "with all holy reverence and attention they wait upon God in that ordinance, diligently observe the sacramental elements and actions, heedfully discern the Lord's body, and affectionately meditate on his death and sufferings, and thereby stir up them-selves to a vigorous exercise of their graces." But that's not all. Recip-ients of the holy meal are also to examine themselves, lament their sins, hunger and thirst for Christ, feed on him in faith, trust his merits, rejoice in his love, give thanks for his grace, and renew "their covenant with God, and love to all the saints" (WLC, art. 174). And this is only what is expected from believers during the administration of the Lord's Supper. Answer 171 of the Larger Cat-echism is equally fulsome in describing the duties of believers in preparing to receive the sacrament, something that happens days before and during the service. Without going into all of the details, the point here is that the ministry of Word and sacrament when properly executed, both by ministers and the laity, is no passive affair. Rather it is strenuous work, even more demanding than the activities of so-called contemporary worship.

Baptism is no less engaging for those who seemingly sit and watch. In the Larger Catechism, the divines speak of the ways in which we are to "improve" our baptism (Q&A 167). Since it is a lifelong duty, baptism is something that touches the believer's daily routine, as the catechism puts it, "especially in the time of temp-tation." In other words, baptism doesn't stop at the time of admin-istration but is a constant aid throughout the Christian walk, thanks to "the privileges and benefits conferred and sealed thereby." But as important as baptism is to a believer's daily devotion, it is par-ticularly conducive to growth in grace during worship. For one of the times in which believers improve their own baptism, no matter how many years ago it may have been performed, is "when we are present at the administration of it to others" (WLC 167). It is at these times during the service that believers should give "serious and thankful consideration of the nature" of baptism, as well as the "ends for which Christ instituted it." In other words, the kind of participation that is required when hearing the sermon is no less necessary when observing a baptism. Worship really is a verb when it consists of Word, sacraments, and prayer.

And Can It Be Boring?

In fact, it would not be difficult to go through all the elements of Reformed worship and find responsibilities for believers that immediately take them from the passive to the active party in worship. If Christians are actually going to hear the Word read and preached, receive the sacraments, sing, confess their faith, pray as a body, and receive God's blessing—if they are going to do any of these things with any measure of genuine faith, love, and obedience—they will not be able to sit by passively. Worship that is Reformed according to the Word, in the words of the first and greatest commandment, demands loving God with all our heart, soul, and mind (Matt. 22:37). If worship is such a soul-wrenching experience, how could it ever be boring?

The real question, then, is not how to make believers more active in worship, but how did Reformed and Presbyterian churches come to a point where members sometimes perceive preaching, the sacraments, prayer, song, Bible reading, and benedictions as boring? If as the author to the Hebrews declares that in worship we come "to Mount Zion and to the city of the living God, the heavenly Jerusalem" (12:22), where we offer "to God acceptable worship, with reverence and awe" because "our God is a consuming fire" (12:28–29 RSV), then historic forms of Christian worship cannot help but be dazzling, even spooky. After all, we go to church not simply to meet with other believers and hear the thoughts of a man who bears the rank of minister, but to meet in a special way the Lord of hosts, the holy and triune God who is a "consuming fire." Worship, accordingly, is far more compelling than the most riveting of musical rhythms or the cleverest of liturgical dramas. It is a time when heaven and earth meet; it is a holy conversation between the Creator of heaven and earth and his redeemed creatures.

Contemporary Presbyterian and Reformed worship suffers not only from forgetting this cosmic dimension of the faithful's assembly, but also from neglect of what the elements of worship do for God's people. Word, sacraments, and prayer not only please God since he has ordained them as the right way to worship him, but also benefit us. As will become clearer in chapters that follow, worship is a means of grace, a time when believers are built up and sustained in the faith. As the Westminster Shorter Catechism says of preaching and the Lord's Supper, through these elements of worship believers are built up in "holiness and comfort," are nourished, and grow in grace (WSC 89, 96). Rather than looking for ways to become more involved in worship, or ways to make the parts of the services more open to church members, a Reformed understanding of worship would suggest that those in the pew should be looking for as many ways as possible to soak in the gospel that God ordained the ministry of the Word, sacraments, and prayer to communicate. In other words, if a problem exists with Reformed worship, if people do not sense that Sunday services reach them where they are, the difficulty may be inappropriate expectations. There is no better model for worship than the act of saving faith, where "we receive and rest upon [Christ] alone for salvation, as he is offered to us in the gospel" (WSC 86). Receiving and resting may be passive activities, but in the economy of Christian salvation, letting others do the work of ministry is by no means a bad or inactive affair.

8

Worship with
Godly Fear

Q Why does the third commandment require the holy and reverent use of God's names, titles, attributes, ordinances, word, and works?

A We "offer to God acceptable worship, with reverence and awe; for our God is a consuming fire."

(Heb. 12:28–29 RSV)

As we have tried to show so far, two principles are crucial to the activities and shape of Reformed worship—the regulative principle and the dialogical nature of corporate worship. The former permits us to do in public worship only what God commands in his revealed Word. The latter, by underscoring the nature of worship as a meeting between God and his people, assigns to the appropriate parties certain roles and functions in the worship service. These two principles inform the *what* (the elements), the *when* (the order), and the *who* (the participants) of worship. Still another important way to apply these principles has to do with the *how* of worship. In other words, the dialogical and regulative principles also have something to say about the tone and mood of worship.

Put another way, we learn from these principles not only what is permissible in worship, but also what is wise in worship. The Bible tells us that we must worship God with fear and sobriety in an orderly way. We do not merely meet God in prayer, Word, song, and sacraments, but we do so in a reverent fashion. So acceptable worship is a dialogue with God that displays awe and godly fear in an appropriate pattern of elements. It is not enough to have the Word of God preached by a properly ordained minister. To conduct these elements with flippancy or carelessness is to offer worship that is as displeasing to God as worship that had improper elements such as tongues and making the sign of the cross, or dance or drama.

John Calvin wrote that "pure and real religion" manifested itself through "faith so joined with an earnest fear of God that this fear also embraces willing reverence."[1] Reverence and fear are at the

heart of Christian worship. But our irreverent age, borrowing frequently from the idioms of Wall Street and Hollywood, has cultivated such informality and false intimacy that it renders any notion
of reverence, much less *willing* reverence, increasingly remote.

For this reason, much of today's worship is oriented, consciously
or not, around the idea of entertainment. Pastors and elders fall
under tremendous pressure to conduct services that are lively, practical, and relevant in order to keep the people in the pews interested in what is happening. The constant fear is that members will
leave a boring style of worship for the church across town with better music, a bigger and younger congregation, and with better lighting and sound systems. Sermons are becoming messages geared
more to "felt" needs than to driving home the needs that the Bible
says fallen men and women (both redeemed and unredeemed)
have. And the message itself is delivered by someone who tries to
come across as a "regular guy," not God's servant who is a steward
of the mysteries of God, who must handle the word of truth with
care, and who has been set apart for this holy task. Writing in the
Christian Century, Edward Farley recently commented that contemporary worship creates a tone that is "casual, comfortable,
chatty, busy, humorous, pleasant and at times even cute." He goes
on to suggest that "if the seraphim assumed this Sunday morning
mood, they would be addressing God not as 'holy, holy, holy,' but
as 'nice, nice, nice.' "[2]

Some defenders of contemporary worship even go so far as to
deny that there is any distinction between the purposes of worship
and the purposes of entertainment. In a recent book tellingly titled
Entertainment Evangelism, one megachurch pastor argues that
effective worship is measured by the extent to which it is good
entertainment. This is because those "raised in an entertainment
age . . . find church to be insufficiently interesting or stimulating."[3]
John M. Frame, in his book *Worship in Spirit and Truth*, puts it
more cautiously when he asserts that worship should take place in
"an informal service with a friendly, welcoming atmosphere and

contemporary styles in language and music."[4] Following this logic, worship style becomes a matter of taste. We would agree, but only if the taste to which he is referring is God's taste. Irreverent worship is a violation of God's holy style. God desires reverent worship, worship that reflects the seriousness that is inherent in a religion that required the death of his only begotten Son in order to redeem a chosen people from the bonds of sin and misery and to deliver them into the glorious blessedness of God's children.

Reverence in the Bible

To understand what Scripture teaches regarding reverence in worship, it is helpful to begin by saying what it is not. First, dignity in worship is not achieved through elaborate ceremonies or complex liturgies. In fact, Calvin believed that "wherever there is great ostentation in ceremonies, sincerity of the heart is rare indeed."[5] And so reverence must always be accompanied by simplicity. It is all too common these days to hear of Christians, even Reformed Christians, who are so fed up with the superficiality and casualness in their services that they take refuge in the Episcopalian or Roman Catholic church. Why have they gone to Canterbury or Rome and not Geneva? Too often these liturgical migrants are motivated by personal taste, except that now their style of worship has become more refined. Candles, incense, banners, and crosses become substitutes for large video monitors, skits, and drums. Both of these forms or styles, we would argue, are at odds with the simplicity peculiar to Reformed worship where the Word, sacraments, and prayer form the substance of activity.

Similarly, reverence is not an argument for elitism. It is just as irreverent to put a symphony orchestra at the front of a church as a rock 'n' roll band. Such displays connote an atmosphere of "entertain the audience," where church members applaud performers and marvel at the musicians' skills, instead of concentrating on

God and his Word. (We will address later how this logic applies to worship music and how it contributes to a sense of reverence.)

Further, there is no universal standard for expressing reverence. For instance, in Asia and other parts of the East, bowing expresses the kind of respect that Westerners usually demonstrate by shaking hands. So too there are a variety of ways for churches to embody reverence, depending on the culture in which they minister and worship. But however it is expressed, reverence must always characterize Christian worship.

Finally reverence does not exclude joy, contrary to the charge of some critics of Reformed worship. Joy—along with a full range of emotions such as grief, anger, desire, hope, fear and love—should find natural outlets in worship. But the need for reverence and gravity dictates that any expression of emotion in worship should be tempered by moderation, self-control, and above all, respect for who God is and an awareness of our place before him.

Having tried to answer common objections to an emphasis on reverence, we would argue that reverent worship simply defined is the necessary consequence of proper theological reflection. The doctrine of God and his holiness and justice, the doctrine of man and his depravity, the doctrine of Christ and his sacrificial atonement, and the doctrine of the Holy Spirit and his effectual application of redemption, together prompt Christians to come into God's presence with holy fear. Perhaps the best definition of reverent worship comes from the Bible itself. Think again, for instance, of the prophet Isaiah's response to God's presence: "Woe is me! For I am lost" (Isa. 6:5 RSV). Isaiah was not adopting a casual pose in a comfortable setting. Moreover, Isaiah's example is not simply a function of Old Testament worship. Revelation also describes reverent worship when in the presence of the Lamb the elders say, "To him who sits upon the throne and to the Lamb be blessing and honor and glory and might for ever and ever," and then those same elders fall down and worship their God (Rev. 5:13–14 RSV).

Since the fall of our first parents, the Old Testament tells us, man could come to God only through the shedding of blood. For the Israelites, sacrifice was synonymous with worship. "Bring an offering, and come before him," we read in 1 Chronicles 16:29 (RSV), the implication being, of course, that you don't come to God without one. This is a pattern that goes all the way back to the beginning of the human race, as the account of Cain and Abel demonstrates (Gen. 4).

As this sacrificial system developed in redemptive history, it culminated in the rules and regulations that were carefully detailed in the book of Leviticus. There God directed his people to worship him through complex layers of ceremony. *Only* clean and spotless animals were to be sacrificed. *Only* priests appointed by God could act as the intercessors between God and his people. *Only* the high priest could offer the highest sacrifices in the holy of holies, *only* on the annual Day of Atonement, *only* when he is properly bathed and attired. The priest was to perform the offerings in a carefully choreographed order that had to be followed with unqualified precision (see Lev. 16).

All of this was a constant reminder of God's holiness and man's sinfulness. Without this scrupulous attention to detail and unwavering obedience to God's instructions, God would find worship unacceptable. The Israelites knew that if God did not consume the sacrifice he would consume the worshipers. God's righteous curse bars our access to him, and God in his capacity as judge is angry toward us. Hence a mediator must intervene, offering a sacrifice on our behalf, in order that his wrath may be appeased and we may obtain his favor. Needless to say, the Old Testament sacrificial system cultivated godly fear and reverence.

In the New Testament, God also requires fear and reverence from those who would worship him in Spirit and in truth. The writer to the Hebrews provides an infallible commentary on Old Testament ceremonial law. All of the "onlys" in Leviticus served to prefigure the fulfillment of God's purposes: *only Christ.* As

Hebrews says, "But when Christ appeared as a high priest of the good things to come, He entered through the greater and more perfect tabernacle, not made with hands, that is to say, not of this creation; and not through the blood of goats and calves, but through His own blood, He entered the holy place once for all, having obtained eternal redemption" (Heb. 9:11–12). The one-and-only, Jesus Christ, the only redeemer of God's elect, fulfilled Israel's rituals. New covenant worshipers enjoy the reality that the Old Testament only foreshadowed. The church has the perfected sacrifice, and that sacrifice provides a better way to worship God.

To be sure, the New Testament proclaims a radical transformation in worship thanks to the saving work of Christ. When the shadows have disappeared and the fulfillment of the types arrives, Christ transforms the cowering fear of God in Leviticus into bold access. Paul writes that through faith in Christ "we may approach God with freedom and confidence" (Eph. 3:12). This idea is echoed in the letter to the Hebrews at several points. "Therefore let us draw near with confidence to the throne of grace," the author writes (4:16). Similarly, he says "we have confidence to enter the holy place by the blood of Jesus" (Heb. 10:19). Thus we can do what the Old Testament believers could not do—we can approach God with boldness and confidence. But we may do so only because of the passion and blood of Jesus Christ.

And so it can be said that in one sense, the whole ceremonial law in Leviticus is obsolete for the Christian (Heb. 8:13). But we must not overlook another sense in which the Levitical rituals are still of abiding relevance. Leviticus provides the theological categories for understanding Christ's priesthood and for our worship through him. The same God who established the sacrificial system for Israel sent his own son as a sacrifice in the fullness of time. Consequently, the principles of worship revealed in Leviticus are still instructive for understanding the manner in which Christians approach God in public worship.

Evangelical Marcionism

Protestants believe that through the perfection of Christ we worship with confidence. But it is precisely on this matter of confidence that confusion usually develops in Protestant worship. When believers first come to Christ, they approach God fearfully. The demands of his law weigh heavily against their souls. The Holy Spirit convicts of sin and misery, and through the mediation of Christ, who has hushed the thunder and quenched the flame of Sinai, believers come to God, not the angry lawgiver, but the loving Father, whom they lovingly and enthusiastically embrace. But that was then at the time of conversion and the early thrill of new faith. After a while, however, as believers come before the Father each week in worship, the service becomes trivial and routine. Worship is regular, almost monotonous, and a sense emerges that fear is no longer a proper emotion since salvation is an ongoing reality. As such, some believers approach God as people without sin, thus allowing for an attitude more casual.

This transformation of worship parallels a problem that afflicted the early church. Marcion was a second-century heretic who maintained a radical difference between the Old and New Testaments, between the God of the Jews, who was vengeful and wrathful, and the Father of Jesus, a God of grace and mercy. Seeing these two as irreconcilably opposed, he reduced the Christian canon to only those portions of the New Testament that spoke of the God of love. Although the early church condemned him, Marcion could be the patron saint of many contemporary Christians because all too often we come to worship thinking like Marcion. Yes, God was strict in the Old Testament; Leviticus tells us that. But he became loving in the New Testament, or so it seems. New Testament worship is no longer formal or strict or highly regulated. The church needs to become informal, spontaneous, and user friendly—words that hardly fit the image of Leviticus.

To follow Marcion is to have a gravely false sense of confidence. It is to remove Christ as the object of our confidence, and thus to twist confidence into presumption. And it is to misunderstand the book of Hebrews. Hebrews warns that the fire of Mount Zion is far greater than the fire of Mount Sinai (12:18–22). Our confidence in our right standing before God, the full assurance that we bring to God in worship, comes only on the basis of Christ's objective work. Yes, we draw near to the Father with "full assurance of faith." This assurance drives out all bondage and fear. But it should not promote indifference, casualness, or presumption. If so, we may be guilty of false assurance.

Confidence and Reverence

Even the most casual of contemporary worship services will be occasionally marked by some sobriety. Most will concede that at least some reverence is required, for example, when the church observes the Lord's Supper. Yet even in these expressions of reverence a false notion prevails. What tends to happen is that worship services toggle back and forth between these seemingly contradictory emotions: a little upbeat praise here, some somber reverence there.

In contrast to such schizophrenia is the language of our Reformed confessions. For example the Westminster Shorter Catechism instructs us when in prayer to "draw near to God *with all holy reverence and confidence*" (Q&A 100). Similarly, the Heidelberg Catechism tells us to come to God our Father in prayer with "childlike reverence for and trust in God" (Q&A 120). Reformed catechisms discourage our imagining that, when coming to the Father with reverence and confidence, we must balance delicately two contradictory sentiments, tightroping between extremes. And so the Belgic Confession contrasts godly fear with "foolish fear," the latter being a fear that is dislocated from the work of Christ (art. 26). Likewise, the Heidelberg Catechism insists that godly fear characterize our use of God's name. It teaches that the third commandment requires that we "not profane or abuse the name of God" but rather that "we use the holy name of God in no other way than with *fear and reverence*, so that He may be rightly confessed and worshipped by us, and be glorified in all our words and works" (Q&A 99). Finally, the Canons of Dort link reverence and joy as complementary, not antagonistic, characteristics. Perseverance works "humility, *reverence*, piety, patience, prayer, endurance in suffering, confession of the truth, and *rejoicing*" (Fifth Head of Doctrine, art. 12). We see then that reverence and confidence are mutually reinforcing. We can be truly confident *because we are reverent*. Likewise, we can be truly reverent *because we are confident*.

The teaching of the Reformed confessions suggests a simple test for distinguishing between genuine and counterfeit joy in worship: Is it accompanied by reverence or not? Are we boasting in our Savior or are we boasting in ourselves? Are we looking to Christ for access to God, or are we feeling good about our own merits? We overcome our fear only through the death and resurrection of Christ. We are spared death and judgment only because Christ willingly submitted to both. How dare we observe Christ's work in any superficial or indifferent or irreverent manner! If we do, we are surely prone to relocate the source of our confidence. If we overcome our fear through any other means than the blood of Christ, we are dangerously close to committing blasphemy.

Indeed, we do not believe that it is putting it too strongly to suggest that Christians come to worship with the same attitude and demeanor they take to a funeral service for a professing Christian. Such funerals are times of reverence and joy. When we contemplate the death of a loved one, we are filled with sadness and are reminded of our own frailty. Yet when the deceased is a believer, the service is also an occasion for joy because we trust that God has called one of his children to be with him, and that the believer has been "made perfect in holiness" and has "passed immediately into glory." Why should a worship service, where the death of our

Lord is central, be any different? His death is one that we caused, death that should provoke hatred for our sin and humility for our unworthiness. This is the ethos of most observances of the Lord's Supper, a fact that may argue for weekly communion in order to ensure reverence in our worship.

Of course, we do not stop with Christ's death in our worship. We go on to rejoice at his resurrection, without which, the apostle says, we would not have hope. Still, the joy we experience in contemplating and worshiping the risen Savior is an emotion that is always tinged with sobriety and humility. It is not the high-fiving ecstasy of fans who have just seen their team win the national championship. Nor is it the celebration of a job promotion. It is a joy that recognizes not only the suffering and death of Jesus Christ, but also our own complicity, because of our sin, in his pain and death. When we contemplate the suffering of Christ we come in humility, restraining sinful impulses, and we embrace a bleeding Savior as the fountain of our comfort.

Of course, reverence is not obviously attractive or appealing. It is hard and uncomfortable. It doesn't create a relaxed or welcoming atmosphere. Above all it is not celebrative as that word has come to be used. Reverent worship is not an effective way of persuading the world that Christians are capable of having a good time. That is because modern culture cannot see God as frightening. So seeker-sensitive worship has replaced a consuming fire with an affirming and empowering God, one who accepts whatever we do. It has substituted the meeting of felt needs for the demands of his law. From this it follows that we no longer need a mediator. Of course, many will say we still need Christ, but their attitude and posture in worship suggest otherwise. When we fail to gather on the Lord's Day to offer unconditional honor to the Savior, we are exchanging true for sham worship. Unfortunately, many contemporary innovations in worship seem to do just that by reflecting an unwarranted confidence in those assembled. As a result, the work of Christ is silenced and pushed to the margins of our life. No longer is his sacrifice our only hope for access to the Father.

By practicing reverence, Christian worship can subvert our therapeutic culture with the truth that God comes to us only on his terms, and never on ours. His terms are the sacrifice. Only in the death and resurrection of Christ do we meet God and escape his wrath and curse. In Christ we find both "the kindness and severity of God" (Rom. 11:22). God accepts our worship because as a consuming fire he has consumed the sacrifice on our behalf.

In the end, reverent worship cultivates the sense that worshipers may offend God and will if they fail to come to him in the ways he has prescribed. Worship should be characterized by godly fear and humility. It is done not lightly but with care and diligence. It is the natural response of creatures in the presence of the holy and sovereign God. And it is worship that conforms to God's Word: "Therefore, since we receive a kingdom which cannot be shaken, let us show gratitude, by which we may offer to God an acceptable service with reverence and awe; for our God is a consuming fire" (Heb. 12:28–29 RSV).

9

The Means
of Grace

Q What are the outward and ordinary means whereby Christ communicates to us the benefits of
redemption?

A The outward and ordinary means whereby Christ communicates to us the benefits of redemption are his ordinances, especially the Word, sacraments, and prayer,
all of which are made effectual to the elect for their salvation.

(Westminster Shorter Catechism, 88)

Earlier we discussed the vertical dimension or the dialogical principle of worship. As we pointed out, worship is for God and not for us. God is the audience of our worship, not unchurched seekers or even fellow believers. He alone is the one whom we are to please in our worship. Worship, then, is not chiefly about evangelism, nor is it a concert, lecture, or counseling session. All of these activities may be legitimate and worthwhile for Christians. But none of them constitutes public worship.

Our focus now turns to what worship does for the church and how it nurtures and edifies believers through the means of grace. But before proceeding, we need to ask whether by looking at what worship does for Christians we are involved in a contradiction. If the sole criterion for public worship is whether God is pleased, isn't it impious, or at least inconsistent, to ask whether and how we as worshipers are blessed? There is no contradiction here because the Bible makes clear that something does indeed happen to participants in worship. When we praise and glorify God, we will be blessed. And the way God blesses his people, the way he causes Christians to grow in grace, is principally through worship that pleases and honors him.

This principle finds expression in Psalm 1. "Blessed is the man," we read, whose "delight is in the law of the LORD" (1:1–2). Growth in grace will come to the believer as he obeys God:

He will be like a tree firmly planted by streams of water,
Which yields its fruit in its season
And its leaf does not whither;
And in whatever he does, he prospers (Ps. 1:3).

Scripture always connects growth in grace with pleasing God. The vertical character of worship, then, contains a blessing for us. We need not add to worship any horizontal elements for our benefit. The Westminster Shorter Catechism spells this out, affirming that God makes preaching, the sacraments, and prayer effectual means of saving his people. In other words, God promises to bless his people through the means of grace.

The catechism also calls these elements of worship "outward and ordinary." They work slowly and quietly in reorienting our hearts heavenward. This is what God has designed for the souls of his people. But these ordinances are not a quick fix, nor do they necessarily produce a spiritual high. Too often, in pursuit of a spirituality of instant gratification, believers miss how useful public worship is in living the Christian life — they look for spiritual things that appear to be more substantial and make a bigger impact. But to miss the blessings of the ordinances that God has ordained is to forget that God is wise and knows what is best. The diet he has prescribed may not satisfy spiritual taste buds that have become accustomed to other forms of devotion. But the diet set before believers in worship is guaranteed to be nourishing because God himself has promised to bless and cause his face to shine upon those who worship him through the means of preaching, sacrament, and prayer.

Consider, for example, the experience of the early church on the Day of Pentecost. In response to Peter's sermon, 3,000 souls came to faith. What then happened to these new Christians? Filled with the Spirit, did they pursue extraordinary experiences of spiritual ecstasy? On the contrary, they attended faithfully to the outward and ordinary means of grace: "They were continually devoting themselves to the apostles' teaching and to fellowship, to the breaking of bread and to prayer" (Acts 2:42). If that was true for the early church at the time of a remarkable event in the unfolding of redemptive history, how can it be otherwise for the church in her current pilgrimage as she awaits the return of her Lord?

Means and Secondary Causes

The language of "the means of grace" should not be foreign to Presbyterians and Reformed. To speak of "means" is simply a way of referring to God's providence. According to the Westminster Shorter Catechism, God's providence is the way he preserves and governs all his creatures and all their actions (Q&A 11). God does not carry out his purposes in history only through miracles or the regeneration of the human soul. Rather he controls all of history through the use of secondary causes. God's providence also extends to the salvation of his people. To be sure, God may intervene and has acted directly in human history by accomplishing mighty deeds to save his people, most notably through the life and ministry of his only begotten Son. But God's redemptive care is not demonstrated only in extraordinarily miraculous displays of his saving power, but also extends to the ordinary means he has ordained for the good of his children.

Presbyterian and Reformed conservatives have been leery of employing the language of means of grace thanks in large part to battles with liberal Protestantism. Because liberal theology tended to reduce all of history to empirically verifiable causes, it often denied the reality of miracles and limited God's power and presence only to his immanence in the forces of creation. Conservatives have battled so hard to defend the transcendence of God and the truth of miracles, that they sometimes overlook the reality of God's providential working through secondary causes. But to affirm with the catechism the legitimacy of means is not to deny supernaturalism. It is simply to acknowledge that God uses all aspects of creation to perform his bidding. God works sovereignly in the lives of all of his saints through circumstances that he ordains.

The doctrine of miracles, then, should not prevent us from recognizing the doctrine of ordinary providence. We should not be afraid to talk about means. The Westminster Confession refers to means in its chapter on providence. "God, in his ordinary providence, makes use of means, yet is free to work without, above, and against them, at his pleasure" (5.3). Providence is one way in which God accomplishes his purposes. This does not mean that it is only through secondary causes that God works (the liberal Protestant error). We are not forced to choose between providence and miracles. God works through both. But sometimes the twentieth-century Protestant church has forgotten that God uses all things to carry out his saving purpose. This is especially important to keep in mind when considering worship, because here God has ordained certain means for the salvation of his people.

Manna in the Wilderness

Worship is our work. But more importantly, it is God's work. In the elements of worship God is at work saving his people. Some may object that believers are already the recipients of God's saving grace, as if his redemptive efforts stop at the time of conversion and justification by faith. The Bible, in fact, teaches that God's people *are* saved, that they *are being* saved, and that they *will be* saved. The means of grace, however, reinforce the idea that the Christians who have converted and are marching toward Zion are *also* weak, frail, sinful, and prone to wander. So we are in constant need of God's grace. And this is what we receive especially in worship.

Perhaps no metaphor is more central to the Bible's description of the Christian life than the idea of pilgrimage. The church is like the Israelites in the wilderness (Heb. 3–4). She is an alien and strange people in this present life (1 Peter 2:11), who seeks a heavenly country (Heb. 11:16) because this world is not her home. As she struggles between her new identity of being hidden with Christ in God (Col. 3:3) and her present earthly or temporary surroundings, she suffers. She has not reached her place of rest because the church is at war both with the sin that continues to torment her and with the principalities (or rulers) and powers of this age (Eph. 6:12). As a pilgrim people, the church needs the

grace that comes through the appointed means God has ordained
for public worship.

The means of grace that God provides in worship are sustenance
for believers. They are what keep us going through the wilderness
of our pilgrimage and warfare. If we avoid them or take them for
granted, we foolishly ignore God's gracious and wise provision.
Moreover, if we trivialize them by preferring means of our own
devising, then it is likely that we do not understand how difficult
the pilgrimage of the Christian life is and how generous is God's
provision.

A low view of worship and what transpires there is not only an
insult to our Creator and Redeemer, who desires praise from his
people. It also misconceives terribly the state of our souls. The
psalmist despairs when he is absent from worship: "As the deer
pants for the water brooks, so my soul pants for You, O God. My
soul thirsts for God, for the living God; when shall I come and
appear before God?" (Ps. 42:1–2). These words are too often sen-
timentalized in contemporary praise choruses. But the psalmist is
actually panicking, and his words are laced with desperation, especially as he contrasts his circumstances with the privilege of worship in his past: "These things I remember and I pour out my soul
within me. For I used to go along with the throng and lead them
in procession to the house of God, with the voice of joy and thanksgiving, a multitude keeping festival" (42:4). Ultimately, the psalmist
locates his assurance in the conviction that he will return to worship. "Hope in God, for I shall again praise Him" (42:5; cf. 42:11).
Similarly, the letter to the Hebrews links the pilgrimage metaphor
with the importance of worship: "Let us hold fast the confession
of our hope without wavering, for He who promised is faithful;
and let us consider how to stimulate one another to love and good
deeds, not forsaking our own assembling together, as is the habit
of some, but encouraging one another; and all the more as you
see the day drawing near" (Heb. 10:23–25).

As the Shorter Catechism notes, the means of grace are ordinary, and too often worshipers equate common with boring. This should not be a surprise. God's people have a history of complaining in the wilderness about his provision of manna. To be sure, God can work extraordinarily, as we pointed out in the previous chapter. The Westminster Confession acknowledges this when it says of God's use of means that he "is free to work without, above, and against them, at his pleasure" (5.3). God is not bound to his means in some mechanical way. But to acknowledge the extraordinary work of God is not to expand our options, thereby allowing us to find means of grace of our own devising. To presume upon that right is to ignore the gracious ways by which he has promised to meet us and enable us to grow in grace.

Corporate Grace

In his recent book *The Church,* Edmund P. Clowney notes that the doctrine of the means of grace points us to the truth that the Christian pilgrimage is a *corporate journey.* "Growth in true holiness," Clowney writes, "is always growth together. It takes place through nurture, through the work and worship of the church."[1] The wilderness experience is a corporate march toward the promised land. For this reason, the outward and ordinary means of grace are ecclesiastical ordinances. They belong to the church, which alone possesses the keys of the kingdom. These ordinances of the church are crucial to salvation. On this basis, the Reformers rightly insisted that outside of the visible church "there is no ordinary possibility of salvation" (WCF 25.2). Public worship is not optional for believers because it is the time when the church chiefly conducts its ministry and work.

Calvin employed the metaphor of motherhood in order to stress the church's vital necessity for Christian life. "Let us learn, even from the simple title 'mother,' how useful, indeed how necessary, it is that we should know [the church]. For there is no other way to enter life unless this mother conceive us in her womb, give us birth, nourish us at her breast, and lastly, unless she keep us under her care and guidance until, putting off mortal flesh, we become like the angels. Our weakness does not allow us to be dismissed from her school until we have been pupils all our lives. Furthermore, away from her bosom one cannot hope for any forgiveness of sins or any salvation." For Calvin, so essential was the church and the means that she provided that he was willing to conclude, "he who refuses to be a son of the Church desires in vain to have God as his Father."[2]

American Protestants generally overlook the communal, and therefore churchly, character of their faith. They commonly practice what some have dubbed "churchless Christianity," where church membership and worship attendance is incidental to the Christian life. Religious polling data have shown that large majorities of American Christians believe that they should arrive at their religious convictions independent of any church. But as Calvin and the Westminster Confession teach, the Reformed tradition rejects the individualism of contemporary American spirituality or any kind of designer spirituality that invites believers to pick and choose what works best. We should not come to church as consumers, looking for the best-equipped nursery or the most dynamic youth program. Instead, we come to church to be discipled by the ministry that Christ gave to his church in the Great Commission (i.e., Word and sacrament).

Moreover, the means of grace are fundamentally corporate in character. When we come to worship, we are not engaging in an individual experience. Public worship is always in the company of the saints, and its activities are for the participation of the whole congregation. For this reason it is inappropriate to sing songs, say prayers, or insist on parts of the service that cater to the devotion of individual believers. If, for instance, we close our eyes and lift our hands in a congregation where no one else does this, we are cutting ourselves off from other worshipers in order to pursue a personal and privatized experience with God. This is one reason why the Westminster divines distinguished between public worship (of the congregation) and private worship (of families or individuals).

Finally, adequate attention to the means of grace should produce greater reluctance to abandon the practice of evening worship. Although the Bible may not specifically prescribe when and how often churches are to gather for worship on the Lord's Day, the idea of worship as a means of grace should challenge the prevailing notion that attendance only at the morning service is sufficient. When we are absent from worship that is called by the elders of our church, are we not neglecting the fullest portion of the blessing that God offers? Isn't the implicit message that we do not need the ministry that the church provides when it assembles for the public proclamation of the Word, for lifting our hearts up in prayer, and for offering praise and thanksgiving to God in song? And when our churches are dark and empty on Sunday evenings, are the elders of the church nourishing their flock as adequately as God would have them?

Benefits of Redemption

Precisely what do the means of grace accomplish? How do they communicate grace to us? The Shorter Catechism, for instance, says that the Word read and especially preached, the sacraments and prayer are the "means by which Christ communicates to us the benefits of redemption" (Q&A 88). What are these benefits? Earlier in the Shorter Catechism, the divines identify these benefits as "justification, adoption, and sanctification" (Q&A 32). As strange as this may sound, there is a sense in which we can say that we are justified, adopted, and sanctified *through worship*. And this is not all. There are additional benefits that "accompany or flow from justification, adoption, and sanctification." These are "assurance of God's love, peace of conscience, joy in the Holy Ghost, increase of grace, and perseverance therein to the end" (Q&A 36).

What more could we need in the pilgrimage and difficulties of the Christian life? What could be more blessed than to receive these benefits on the Lord's Day when throughout the week we experience suffering and persecution, and fight the residue of sin and temptations of the flesh? What could be more comforting than to receive God's blessing? And how else are we to obtain his mercy and reassurance than through the diligent use of the means of grace?

The instrumentality of worship in communicating these benefits is explained in the Shorter Catechism. It is "the Spirit of God" who makes "the reading, but especially the preaching, of the Word, an effectual means of convincing and converting sinners, and of building them up in holiness and comfort, through faith, unto salvation" (Q&A 89). This is a bold claim. But it is exactly what Paul teaches when he writes that faith comes through hearing the preached Word of God (Rom. 10:13–15). This also seems like an archaic claim. In a media-saturated and increasingly visually-oriented culture, communication experts are telling church leaders that the sermon is an ineffective and outmoded means of communication. After all, people cannot devote sustained attention to anything, much less a "talking head," for more than five to ten minutes. Yet here the church must be countercultural and trust in the promises of God, even if it appears foolish according to the wisdom of our age. As Paul also writes, ". . . God was well-pleased through the foolishness of the message preached to save those who believe" (1 Cor. 1:21). Ultimately, the work of salvation belongs to the agency of the Holy Spirit who applies Christ's work of redemption. So too the effectiveness of preaching depends not on the pastor but on God. Relying on "foolish" means is nothing more than trusting in the power of God.

What is said here of preaching applies to the other means of grace. They also convince and convert, and sustain us in the faith.

Baptism, the Shorter Catechism says, is a "partaking of the benefits of the covenant of grace" (Q&A 94). Moreover, in the Lord's Supper believers "are . . . made partakers of his body and blood, with all his benefits, to their spiritual nourishment, and growth in grace" (Q&A 96). Notice again the language of benefits. Believers receive these benefits through the means God has appointed.

In this teaching the Westminster divines are simply following Calvin. He wrote that "the sacraments bring the clearest promises; and . . . they represent [the Word] for us as painted in a picture from life."[3] The sacraments, Calvin argues, are sermon illustrations from God. They are the images he uses to show us the gospel. Moreover they confirm us in the good news of God's saving promises. According to Calvin baptism and the Lord's Supper, along with the Word read and preached, "have been instituted by the Lord to the end that they may serve to establish and increase faith."[4]

Finally, prayer as a means of grace also comes with the promise of God's blessing. When we offer up our requests to God for things agreeable to his will, then our prayers will be a blessing to us and cause us to grow in grace. This can happen, of course, in private prayer. But corporate prayer knits the hearts of church members together. The Lord's Prayer is a "we" prayer, a model for praying together, with and for others.

But the Word, sacraments, and prayer do not become means of grace on their own. We are not advocating the Roman Catholic idea that the sacraments or other ordinances confer grace whenever a man rightly ordained performs them, that is, sacerdotalism. Instead, what we are talking about is the communication of grace through means that ultimately depend for their efficacy on the ministry of the Holy Spirit. The Spirit accompanies the preaching of the Word. The Spirit enables the spiritual presence of Christ in the sacraments. And the Spirit prays with us, translating our groanings into words pleasing to God and edifying to us. The Reformers stressed the work of the Spirit in order to avoid the errors of Rome.

Grace is not dispensed by any virtue in the means themselves or in those who administer them, as if by some automatic or magical way. Rather, grace only comes as God works through these means. The reassuring teaching, though, is that our loving and merciful God has ordained these means for the good of the ones whom he has graciously saved. Ultimately, the means of grace are only effective through "the blessing of Christ, and the working of his Spirit in them that by faith receive them" (WSC Q&A 91).

Effectual for Salvation

We are not saying here that God will not provide us with assurance of his love or an increase in grace through other means. Christians may find comfort and aid through listening to Christian radio or participating in small-group Bible studies. God can always work wherever and whenever he pleases. But the Bible does teach that God has promised to bless the means of grace that he provides in worship in a way that he has not promised to bless anything else. We have no need to expect God to work through anything else if we attend diligently to the means he has promised to bless. If we want God's blessing, if we want genuine comfort for the difficulties of our pilgrimage, then we have no further to look than the outward and ordinary means. The means communicated through the church are made effectual to the saints for their salvation. To take the Word, sacraments, and prayer for granted—in other words, to disregard public worship as something to be added on to personal devotions or small-group fellowship—is to trivialize worship and put ourselves at risk.

Dieters know how dubious are the promises of many heavily advertised weight-loss programs. God's diet is a sure thing. The Spirit promises to make these outward means effectual for our salvation. God honors his own promises and uses the Word, sacraments, and prayer to save. No such divine blessing is promised for wearing "What Would Jesus Do" bracelets or listening to Amy

Grant sing "Father's Eyes." So the choice comes down to eating the manna of God's gracious provision or supping on the food of our own creation. And to make that choice, we need to see how great God's provision is for us in worship, and how important it is to our own spiritual health and well being. The means of grace are part and parcel of Christian worship. We worship to praise God and to give him the glory that he alone deserves. And in worship, through the means of grace, God is also at work, extending his blessing to his people, and transforming us into his image.

10

Elements, Circumstances, and Forms

What are the elements of Christian worship?

The reading of the Scriptures with godly fear; the sound preaching, and conscionable hearing of the Word, in obedience unto God with understanding, faith, and reverence; singing of psalms with grace in the heart; as, also, the due administration . . . of the sacraments instituted by Christ; are all parts of the ordinary religious worship of God. . . .

(Westminster Confession of Faith, 21.5)

Our discussion of worship thus far has been relatively abstract, or lacking in specific examples. We have looked, for instance, at the regulative principle for worship, the dialogical character of worship, and the obligation to worship God with reverence and awe. Much of this material assumes an understanding of the basic parts or elements of worship. In fact, the closest we have come in the book to a sustained discussion of the actual components of a worship service was in the previous chapter on the means of grace. But even there our presentation stopped with an argument for the Word, sacraments, and prayer as the central features of Christian worship. Most people agree that worship should consist of preaching, praying, and song. But are all of these things essential for worship? Can what takes place be worship if these activities do not occur? Is anything else required? These questions find useful answers in the distinctions that our confessional standards draw among the elements, circumstances, and forms of worship.

Presbyterian Worship

From what we have studied so far, it should be evident that the challenge of determining the proper features of worship is distinctive to Presbyterians and Reformed. It is not a Catholic or Lutheran or Episcopalian problem, because Reformed alone approach worship from the perspective of the regulative principle. Reformed believe that church sessions and consistories must protect the consciences of worshipers by not requiring anything in worship beyond biblical mandate. Reformed worship, therefore, was simple, orderly, and reverent, and the people of God came into God's presence in a manner that has endeavored to follow the practices of the early church.

Evelyn Underhill noted the distinctiveness of Reformed worship in her 1937 study on worship. "No organ or choir," she wrote, "was permitted in [Calvin's] churches; no color, nor ornament but a table of the Ten Commandments on the wall. No ceremonial acts or gestures were permitted. No hymns were sung but those derived from a biblical source." She goes on to note the distinctive character of Reformed church architecture. The walls were whitened, and the pulpit was at the center, along with the baptismal font and table. Unlike Catholic, Lutheran, or Episcopalian worship, the pulpit was not on the side with an altar in the middle.[1]

What drove the starkness of Reformed worship was the conviction that worship that included unbiblical embellishments was a violation of the regulative principle. As the Westminster Confession puts it, "the acceptable way of worshiping the true God is instituted by himself, and so limited by his own revealed will, that he may not be worshiped according to the imaginations and devices of men, or the suggestions of Satan, under any visible representation, or any other way not prescribed in the holy Scripture" (21.1).

Calvin described two advantages to worship regulated in this manner: "First, it tends greatly to establish [God's] authority that we do not follow our own pleasure, but depend entirely on his sovereignty; and secondly, such is our folly, that when we are left at liberty, all we are able to do is to go astray. And then when once we have turned aside from the right path, there is no end to our wanderings, until we get buried under a multitude of superstitions."[2]

Still, the effort to worship God without relying on human wisdom or sincerity, as central as that has been to the Reformed tradition, does not settle the order or components of the service. As we have asserted before, the New Testament does not include a set liturgy like that which God prescribed for Israel in the Old Testament. Congregations need to infer from biblical teaching what to do in worship and in what order. One way to establish a framework for considering the specifics of worship is to use the categories of elements, circumstances, and forms. These designations add a valuable measure of clarity for considering the actual behavior and conduct of believers in worship.

Elements

What features are essential for Reformed worship? Champions of innovation in worship are quick to claim that there is no New Testament book of Leviticus with an explicit manual on the conduct of worship. But there are a host of texts in the New Testament that provide sufficient guidance on proper elements of worship, either from apostolic teaching (such as an explicit command from Paul in his letters), or from apostolic example (the way, for example, that Luke might describe worship during the missionary journeys of Paul). Acts furnishes us with a helpful outline: "They were continually devoting themselves to the apostles' teaching and to fellowship, to the breaking of bread and to prayer" (2:42). Here we find several keys to worship: the Word, prayer, sacraments, and a collection (*koinonia*). Other New Testament texts reiterate that these four elements characterized the worship of the early assemblies of the church on the Lord's Day and that God approved of them. In explaining this text, T. David Gordon writes: "It is not difficult to conclude that the elements which are anticipated by our Lord's instructions to the disciples, which are observed in the churches under apostolic oversight, which are regulated by inspired epistle, are the ministry of the Word, the administration of the sacraments, spoken and sung prayers and praises, and collections for the relief of the saints."[3]

Gordon is echoing Calvin himself, who wrote, "No meeting of the church should take place without the Word, prayers, partaking of the Supper, and almsgiving."[4] Because he saw communion as an element of worship, Calvin went as far as to say that the Reformed church in Geneva should observe the Lord's Supper on every Lord's Day. He was not able to persuade Geneva's authorities to follow his wishes, and Presbyterian and Reformed churches have traditionally celebrated the supper quarterly. Recently, however, many churches are accelerating the frequency of observance, not simply because of the early church's practice but also because of the benefits of the Lord's Supper itself.

Perhaps most difficult to understand among the elements of worship is the offering. Lately many churches, especially the seeker-sensitive ones, are removing the offering from worship. The momentum to do this gained strength in the wake of recent and highly publicized financial scandals among prominent ministers and televangelists. So churches want to avoid creating an impression among visitors that they are more interested in folks' wallets than their souls. But this is an unfortunate confusion of the nature of an offering. The apostle Paul instructs us that the offering is an opportunity to worship and serve God through an expression of thanksgiving (Rom. 12:13), and he reiterates this doctrine in his instruction to the Corinthians to take a collection on the Lord's Day. Paul writes: "Now concerning the collection for the saints, as I directed the churches of Galatia, so do you also. On the first day of every week each one of you is to put aside and save, as he may prosper. . . ." (1 Cor. 16:1–2).

The essentials for Reformed worship, then, are the reading and preaching of the Word, prayer, song, the collection, and the sacraments. To leave these out of worship or to add to them is to go beyond God's Word. Since the aim of worship is to please God, we may not appeal to any other source to discover what pleases him, for example, by speculating on what people may like in worship. Of course, much confusion about worship would be eliminated if worship were properly understood as directed by God and governed by his Word.

Circumstances and Forms

The establishment of the proper elements of worship does not resolve all worship questions. Sessions and consistories need to determine how and when the elements should be carried out in worship. The Bible, for instance, does not say much about the time of worship, the length of worship, or the dimensions and seating capacity of the place where Christians gather. Should a church worship in its own property, in a rented building, or in a home? Should the service be at 8:00 a.m. or 11:00 a.m.? And should worship last all morning? All of these considerations are circumstantial, and the church must decide these matters on the basis of prudence or wisdom. The Westminster Confession acknowledges this when it says, ". . . there are some circumstances concerning the worship of God, and government of the church, common to human actions and societies, which are to be ordered by the light of nature, and Christian prudence, according to the general rules of the Word, which are always to be observed" (1.6).

There is yet another distinction that we need to make to add even greater clarity to the components of a worship service. Consider the definition of worship that is found in the Westminster Confession: "The light of nature shows that there is a God, who has lordship and sovereignty over all; is good, and does good unto all; and is therefore to be feared, loved, praised, called upon, trusted in, and served, with all the heart, and with all the soul, and with all the might"(21.1). Here we have a statement about the kinds of feelings or emotions that characterize true worship: we should express fear, love, praise, and trust. These emotions should inform and envelop all of the elements of worship.

The dimension of worship that is suggested by the confession here is its *form*, or the "how" of the preaching, praying, and singing in worship. The Scriptures do not provide specific forms for public worship. As the *Directory for Worship of the Orthodox Presbyterian Church* states, "The Lord Jesus Christ has prescribed no fixed forms for public worship but, in the interest of life and power in worship, has given his church a large measure of liberty in this matter."[5] Yet, the *Directory* hastens to add, this is a liberty that is to be used wisely: "It may not be forgotten, however, that there is true liberty only where the rules of God's Word are observed and the Spirit of the Lord is, that all things must be done decently and in order, and that God's people should serve him with reverence and in the beauty of holiness." So the church must design its form of worship to enable it to be conducted "properly and in an orderly manner" (1 Cor. 14:40).

The Westminster divines refer implicitly to forms in their Larger Catechism: "Q. What rule has God given for our direction in the duty of prayer? A. The whole Word of God is of use to direct us in the duty of prayer; but the special rule of direction is that form of prayer which our Savior Christ taught his disciples, commonly called the Lord's Prayer" (Q&A 186). The divines suggest here that one particularly useful *form* of prayer is the Lord's Prayer. Similarly the Scriptures instruct us that psalms are appropriate *forms* of song. Reformed and Presbyterian directories for worship describe other forms that should accompany the elements of worship. Regarding the reading of Scripture the OPC *Directory* writes that "the minister does well to refrain from interspersing the reading of God's Word with human comments, and the congregation should attend to the reading with deepest reverence."[6]

Reformed directories have also typically given instructions about the form of the sermon. For instance the OPC *Directory* says that since God addresses the congregation in the sermon by the mouth of his servant, "it is a matter of supreme importance that the minister preach only the Word of God, not the wisdom of man, that he declare the whole counsel of God, and that he handle aright the Word of truth." It also says that sermons must be prepared, a warning to extemporaneous preachers, and that "no person enter the pulpit concerning whose doctrinal soundness or knowledge of Scripture there is reasonable doubt." No topical preaching is allowed, since "in the sermon the minister should explain the Word of God for the instruction of his hearers and then apply it for their exhortation." Life cannot be divorced from doctrine. Sermons should also "warn the congregation of prevalent soul-destroying teachings by enemies of the gospel." Finally the minister should not forget the lost. He should "beseech the unconverted to be reconciled to God . . . in order that the unsaved may rely for salvation on the grace of God only, to the exclusion of their own works or character, and that the saints may ascribe glory for their salvation to God alone."[7] All of these considerations pertain to the form of the sermon. Preaching is not simply what the minister says at the point of the service where the bulletin reads "message." It is an element of worship where God speaks to his people through his undershepherds, and it should assume a fitting form.

And so we have three categories for delineating the parts of a worship service: elements, circumstances, and forms. They pertain to the what, when, and how of worship. *That* we sing in worship is established because song is an element of worship. *How often* we sing in worship is a circumstance to be determined by the session's prudential judgment. *What* we sing in worship— whether psalms or hymns—is a form of worship. The same may be said of the other elements.

These distinctions are very useful for clarifying some of the issues in the so-called worship wars. In some cases, people are simply debating what form to use—a read prayer or one said by the minister, a hymn or a praise song. These may be legitimate debates. But illegitimate ones come when people introduce new elements such as dance and drama. Perhaps some of the debating would be eliminated if these distinctions were kept in mind.

Ritualism: Good or Bad?

Unhappily, attention to the proper form of worship has suffered from neglect in current discussions of worship. One consequence of this inattention is that many Presbyterians are suspicious of liturgy or ritual. Charles Hodge himself wrote that liturgical worship tends "to formality, and cannot be an adequate substitute for the warm outgoings of the heart moved by the spirit of genuine devotion."[8] Thus, the prevailing sentiment is that worship without form, or nonliturgical worship, is the most genuine expression of worship that Christians can offer. Yet a dangerous assumption lurks behind reasoning like this, namely, that genuine devotion and sincere feelings for God can only be expressed adequately when we use our own words, not the words of someone else.

Of course, the charismatic movement has encouraged us to believe that we must worship God in our own tongue, preferring spontaneity and individual expressiveness in worship. We have already noted that charismatics, whatever flaws they may possess, at least have the virtue of worshiping in ways that are consistent with their theology. But Reformed and Presbyterians may not worship like charismatics, or Roman Catholics for that matter. We do not believe that the Holy Spirit works best when we feel a certain way, when we get excited, or when we are caught up in the moment. Nor do we believe that grace is automatically conferred when the sacraments are administered by a priest properly ordained.

To be sure, no one is advocating a return to Rome. Charismatic worship is another matter. And even though charismatics are consistent, their worship rests on several flawed assumptions. First, it is possible for people to be "moved" in worship that follows the Anglican Book of Common Prayer or even the Roman Catholic mass. Many in these communions feel that the Holy Spirit is particularly present when those forms are used. If the emotion of the worshiper is our sole standard, why then is the experience of one reciting the Heidelberg Catechism any less legitimate than that of the person who speaks in tongues? Moreover, what about the experience of the Jew or the Mormon or the Buddhist? If they have a moving experience is their worship more genuine and therefore more true? Obviously not. So ecstasy or spontaneity in worship cannot be a measurement of its legitimacy. The only genuine experience in worship is a proper response to God as he has revealed himself in his Word.

Further, it is possible for worshipers to deceive others and themselves through counterfeit experience. Former Pentecostals have admitted that they have spoken in tongues because they yielded to peer pressure, not necessarily because the Spirit was alive and present. Others have also responded to invitations at the end of evangelistic rallies for less than genuine reasons. Consider too how often extemporaneous prayers are really full of stock expressions and formulas, such as "we just praise you." These examples suggest that some actions that appear spontaneous are really established liturgies in themselves. So there is no avoiding ritual in worship. We are creatures of habit. If habits are useful during the week, why not on the Lord's Day? Moreover, we have been created with souls *and* bodies. As long as we have bodies our worship will be embodied in some manner. Worship, then, must not neglect the physical for the spiritual. Otherwise, the best worship might be some form of transcendental meditation.

Finally, consider the consequences of the modern bias against forms for our doctrine of Scripture. If we use the Bible to pray or to sing praise, are we actually doing something less genuine in our devotion and piety? If we repeat the Lord's Prayer are we guilty of ritualism? And what does spontaneity do to the memorization of Scripture or the catechism? If we use the words of the Bible or the catechism to express our convictions, our desires, our praise and adoration, are we guilty of dead formalism and quenching the movement of the Spirit? Conversely, might not the decline of psalm singing and catechism memorizing among Presbyterians indicate the triumph of experience in our worship?

So forms matter. There is no escaping them. Instead of avoiding them (which is impossible), we need to determine what the correct forms are. They are the forms that please God, that permit us to express the truths he has revealed. Whatever our experience is, these forms are ones that edify us, that build us up in the faith and increase our knowledge and understanding of God's Word.

Does It Matter?

With a proper understanding of elements, circumstances, and forms, let us return to the question of what makes Reformed worship unique. Look, for example at a typical Roman Catholic service:

Introit
Entrance of Clergy
Salutation
Epistle
Gospel
Sermon
Nicene Creed
Salutation
Consecration of Elements
Communion
Thanksgiving
Dismissal

At first glance, we might wonder what is so objectionable about the Roman Catholic liturgy. Aren't the right elements there? There are singing, prayer, and preaching. But are the circumstances proper, when Catholics worship in highly ornamental cathedrals with banners and images that violate the second commandment as Reformed have understood it? And what about the forms? Presbyterians use forms different from Catholic forms. Presbyterians do not raise the bread to consecrate it. They sit at a table, while the Catholics come forward to an altar. A ten-minute homily is a form that does not give significant attention to the Word of God.

We can apply the same critique to contemporary worship styles. These services also seem to include all the proper elements of worship. They have lots of singing, some prayer, and some form of biblical exposition. But are the circumstances biblical when worship takes place on Wednesday night? And is the Word of God received with reverence when the message is communicated through the forms of multimedia?

These distinctions among elements, circumstances, and forms lie at the heart of a proper understanding of worship. Reformed and Presbyterians cannot simply worry about theology and forget about the form theology takes in worship. Elements, circumstances, and forms together produce distinctively Reformed worship, worship that is Reformed according to the Word of God. The result, Terry Johnson writes, is worship that is simple, spiritual, and substantial:

> [It is] *simple* because the New Testament does not prescribe a complex ritual of service as is found in the Old Testament; *spiritual* because when Jesus removed the special status of Jerusalem as *the* place where God was to be worshiped (John 4:7–24), he signaled the abolition of all the material forms that constituted the typological Old Testament system including not only the city, but all that gave the city significance—the temple, the altars, the priests, the sacrificial animals, the incense; *substantial* because the God of the Bible is a great God and cannot be worshiped appropriately with forms that are light, flippant, or superficial; he must always be worshiped with 'reverence and awe' (Hebrews 12:28).[9]

Rather than worshiping in ways indistinguishable from other Protestants, Reformed and Presbyterian services must be evidently different because of what the Reformed tradition has taught and understood about the differences among elements, circumstances, and forms. At the same time, if Reformed worship today is indistinguishable from that of other Protestant communions, it could be the result of other churches reforming their ways and becoming more Reformed. More likely, though, is the explanation that Reformed and Presbyterian churches have adopted the theology and forms of Protestants outside the Reformed fold. Theology (content) and worship (form) cannot be separated. For Reformed churches to retain the theology that has been the genius of Calvinism, they must also maintain forms of worship that have historically made Reformed worship so obvious to spot.

11

Song
in Worship

 **For whom does the church sing in worship?**

O sing to the LORD a new song, for he has done marvelous things! His right hand and his holy arm have gotten him victory.

(Ps. 98:1 RSV)

As we turn our attention to music, we come at last to the most divisive issue in the so-called worship wars. While there is some debate over the other elements of worship—does the offering offend seekers or should the sermon be supplemented with drama?—the heart of the current controversy lies primarily in the selection of music for congregational song. In large measure the worship wars are really wars about singing, with sides divided between "traditionalists," who defend hymns of the eighteenth and nineteenth centuries, and advocates of "contemporary music," who insist on the use of praise songs from the 1970s and 1980s. A visit to representative Presbyterian and Reformed churches will indicate who is winning this war. Increasingly, contemporary choruses and praise songs are replacing hymns in the same way that hymns drove out the metrical psalms over the course of the nineteenth century.

This debate is understandable because the church has long understood the value and necessity of song in worship. Luther said that music was a gift of God that had "the natural power of stimulating and arousing the souls of men."[1] In congregational song worshipers give voice to their beliefs and theology, Luther also noted. And so to sing in worship is to gain a theological education. Calvin likewise stressed the power of music: "We know from experience that song has great force and vigor to arouse and inflame the hearts of men to invoke and praise God with a more vehement and ardent zeal." He went on to warn that music must be selected with great care.

> Wherefore that much more ought we to take care not to abuse it, for fear of fouling and contaminating it, convert-

161

ing it to our condemnation, when it was dedicated to our profit and welfare. If there were no other consideration than this alone, it ought indeed to move us to moderate the use of music, to make it serve everything virtuous, and that it ought not to give occasion for our giving free reign to licentiousness, or for our making ourselves effeminate in disorderly delights, and that it ought not to become an instrument of dissipation or of any obscenity.[2]

What the churches are fighting over, then, is something that is an important part of worship, and something that is vitally connected to our theology. Neither side is disputing the importance of song in worship. Both sides want to sing "with grace in the heart." So neither is violating the regulative principle (assuming that the regulative principle permits music other than the Psalter). For this reason we need to exercise Christian prudence and discernment in determining what is proper song in worship. This is why we have placed the subject at the end of the book. Proper reflection on the appropriate songs for worship may only occur after considering the larger teaching of the Reformed tradition on the holy assembly of saints on the Lord's Day with their covenant God.

Psalms and Hymns

Before we review those principles, a word about psalmody might be in order. The prevailing illiteracy over the Psalter in today's churches is a testimony to how much of our Reformed heritage we have abandoned. Reformed worship ought at least to embrace frequent or even preponderant use of the Psalter. How many of us can claim that we know the Psalms well enough or that we sing them often enough? This is especially worth asking when we see that much traditional hymnody and many contemporary choruses are filled with emotion. The Psalms, interestingly enough, are filled with just as much emotion. But what makes the Psalter's songs and poems different is that they express the emotions to which God has given his blessing, through the inspiration of the Holy Spirit. Psalms not only provide an emotional outlet for which Calvinists are not always well known, but also instill the hearts of saints with godly emotions.

The command found throughout Scripture to "sing a new song" has often been misunderstood and abused. It is important to understand what these words mean. These words are not proof-texts for contemporary music, nor do they mean that the church must always be experimenting or innovating in its song. We should not privilege the new because it is new. On the contrary, a wise approach would be to suspect anything that has not stood the test of time. Instead, to "sing a new song" is to make sure that the hymnody of the church accurately reflects the fullness of God's words and deeds in all stages of redemptive history. As the mighty acts of God unfold in the salvation of his people, the people of God respond with song. There were songs at the exodus (Exod. 15) and at the conquest (Deut. 32). This pattern recurs throughout the Psalms (33:3; 96:1; 98:1; 149:1), and it will characterize worship in the consummated order at the end of time (Rev. 5:9; 14:3).

Churches that only sing from the Psalter, then, need to have a good understanding of the Old Testament and how it reveals Christ. To be sure, this is not easily done. But the early church did sing psalms, and therefore it is possible to sing them from the perspective of redemptive-historical fulfillment. Whatever we sing, our music must reflect the proper response to God's redemptive and self-revelatory acts. Our songs should link together promise and fulfillment, and so the Psalter becomes the pattern for our hymnody. Hughes Oliphant Old put it well when he wrote that hymnody at its best "springs from" psalmody; it "comments on, interprets, and continues the psalmody."[3]

Congregational Song

At this point it might be helpful to review the principles of a Reformed theology of worship that should inform congregational singing. We began the book by describing the antithesis between the church and the world. Nowhere is the church's opposition to the world more pronounced than when it is engaged in public worship. Worship is the church's renunciation of the world. We sing to a God that the world refuses to acknowledge, and so we sing in a way that the world cannot comprehend.

It is easy to detect worldliness in the lyrics of our songs. Songs about romantic love or our favorite sports are clearly inappropriate in public worship. But what about the "music text" to our songs? As fundamentalist as it sounds, there is such a thing as worldly music. Music that is performed at rock concerts or sung in lounges and bars, and even music performed in symphony halls is worldly. That is, it is the world's music. It is designed for appreciation or consumption in worldly settings. Some of it may be better than others, but the world's music should not be the model for the church's song. One lesson this principle teaches is that the church needs to give more attention to her music, and a way to do this may be commissioning musicians to write melodies that are appropriate for public worship and that fit the texts congregations use to praise God.

A point related to the antithesis between the church and the world is that the purpose of the church is discipleship and not merely soul-winning. Therefore, congregational song should edify the people of God. We should not use music as a vehicle to attract outsiders or to appeal to the unchurched. We do not lower our musical standards in order to reach the unsaved, but we raise them so that God's people will grow in the faith. At the same time, song is something that everyone in the congregation is called to do. So the music that churches use should be as accessible as possible to the whole congregation. The rich harmonies of a Bach cantata, then, would be just as difficult for many believers as are the syncopated rhythms of the Newsboys.

Another point that should guide song in worship is the Sabbath. Worship takes place on the Lord's Day, a holy day set apart from the rest of the week, for activities that should be different from what we do on the other six days. This includes music. We should not expect to listen to, much less to sing, the music that we enjoy during the week, a point that applies wherever our tastes may lie, from country to classical to "contemporary Christian music." For this reason, Calvin hired musicians to compose tunes that were fitting for congregational singing on the Lord's Day. Several of Louis Bourgeois' tunes are still in Presbyterian and Reformed hymnals. Again, churches today would do well to follow Calvin in this example rather than letting the music industry (whether Christian or not) set the standards for congregational song.

Another idea we have considered in this book is that of reverence appropriate for gathering in God's presence. Godly fear should characterize our song, in both words and melody. We need to ask whether a given hymn or praise song can cultivate the sensibilities of reverence, along with self-control, discipline, and moderation. This applies especially to much contemporary Christian music that borrows heavily from the musical idiom of rock. One recent commentator on contemporary mass culture argued that rock's forms are at odds with what American Protestants used to identify as Christian virtues. Those virtues were "responsibility, fidelity, sobriety, and other badges of maturity." Instead, "the cumulative message of the rock culture" consists of "sexual and narcotic gratification, anarchism, self-pity, and other forms of infantilism."[4] Of course, not all rock is the same, and "soft" rock is widely popular and has informed much contemporary Christian music. Still, it is valuable to ask whether rock in any form is appropriate for worship if our services are to be marked by reverence and awe. In other words, do our tunes contradict our words? Is it really possible for rock music, whether hard or soft, to be fitting for worship?

The covenant, as we have also argued, governs worship by establishing a dialogical structure for the parts of the service. In turn, congregational song must observe this aspect of Reformed worship. God speaks, and singing is part of our response to his Word. In fact, Calvin argued that worship consisted of three major parts, the Word (read and preached), the sacraments, and prayer. For him, as for many in the Reformed tradition, song was chiefly a form of prayer. It was not, as many argue today, a way of teaching the Word in order to communicate theology. Instead, song in worship is a vehicle for expressing prayerful desires to God. As Psalm 98:1 tells us, we are to sing our songs to God. Because God is the audience for our singing, music should not have a performance component to it, as in special music where the choir or soloist is singing music that one might hear in a concert. The dialogical principle, then, raises an important question for music in worship. Is the choir singing to God on behalf of the congregation or ministering to the congregation as an ambassador of God? And if song is a form of prayer, and if ministers are the ones given the task of leading prayer in public worship, is it proper for one part of the congregation, which has not been ordained, to lead in prayer for the rest of the church? Reformed worship must reflect more carefully on how special music fits within the dialogical principle of Reformed worship. It is still possible to use choirs before worship, to set the tone, or to sing antiphonally with the congregation in order to assist everyone in the church. So our point here is not to prohibit special music. It is to be more careful on the basis of Reformed teaching about worship.

Another doctrine that we have emphasized is that of the regulative principle, the idea that the only kind of acceptable worship is that which pleases God according to his revelation in Scripture. Acceptable worship does not come naturally to sinful people. Worship involves habits and appetites that are only acquired over time by believers as they mature in the faith by exposure to the means of grace. Just as Israel in the wilderness harkened for the diet of

Egypt, we may yearn for the music of this world. But such yearning does not justify the use of such song. Growth in grace will actually elevate our understanding of singing as we are better able to discern what songs are appropriate for the assembly of the saints in worship.

These are some of the ideas that should inform the way Reformed and Presbyterian congregations address the role of music in worship. These Reformed principles show that worship, contrary to much public opinion, is not a matter of taste. It is a matter of theological conviction. In song we give musical expression to the faith we profess. And so, the songs that Presbyterians and Reformed sing in worship should be as distinctive as the theology they hold dear.

True, Good, and Beautiful

But some may object to the notion that only some forms of Christian song are appropriate music for worship. What constitutes good music? Isn't it hard to apply Paul's standards of purity, loveliness, and excellence (Phil. 4:8) to music since those characteristics are not readily evident in melodies, harmonies, and rhythm? In the end, doesn't the selection of worship music boil down to personal preference?

To appreciate how dangerous this common claim is, consider its application in a setting very different from worship. Multiculturalism is a popular doctrine that regards standards for evaluating cultural expression as simply the concoction of the most dominant and powerful groups in society—a case of elites imposing their preferences on everyone else. Consequently, in college and university English literature departments across the country, Shakespeare is being supplanted by a host of new authors who are allegedly more representative of American culture's egalitarian and democratic ways. These formerly silenced voices include women, African-Americans, gays, and lesbians, whose works need to be rediscovered, because students today are no longer made up of white men who enjoy reading the works of other white men such as Shakespeare. Instead, college students now include women, African-Americans, gays, and lesbians, who need to read authors with whom they can identify and whose writings affirm and empower them. Accordingly, the criteria for good literature have shifted from aesthetic or literary grounds, to therapeutic and demographic ones based on the reader's gender, race, or sexual identity. According to today's multiculturalists, good literature cannot transcend race, class, and gender but is only a function of the reader's physical traits or inclinations.

When academic traditionalists counter that the new works being taught are simply not as good as Shakespeare or Milton, they invariably meet the response that they are elitists, who force their own prejudiced standards of the true, the good, and the beautiful on others. The logic of multiculturalism insists that there are no longer any objective and nonarbitrary criteria for valuing some works of literature above others. Instead, the works studied must appeal to those in the classroom. And since universities now revel in diversity, the curriculum cannot be homogenous.

Conservative Protestants are generally on the side of the cultural traditionalists in these debates. They defend the traditional canon, the traditional family, and other traditional values. They make William Bennett's books on virtues bestsellers, and they oppose political correctness in the academy. In fact, they wage this defense vigorously, for six days of the week. But ironically when some of them gather for worship something very different happens. They suddenly display the same hostility to tradition and to aesthetic standards that they deplore in the secular world. For in many Reformed and Presbyterian churches a logic similar to multiculturalism is at work. Some argue that the old hymns and choir anthems are elitist and appeal only to a certain generation of saints who happen in many cases to occupy most positions of leadership. But now the churches have a new generation of Christians who require their own style of music. And if they do not find their music in worship, they will be alienated and ostracized. They won't be able to go to church with a sense that they belong.

Worship for most Christians today, in other words, has become a license for aesthetic relativism. Good music doesn't transcend generation, gender, or region; therefore, churches should use music that appeals to the demographics of their membership. There may be standards for truth and for morality, but there do not appear to be any clear ones for music or song. The mindset of many appears to be that believers should look for a congregation that worships in a way that makes them feel comfortable.

All of this is not to deny that cultural considerations come to bear on our music. The *form* that the elements of worship take, music included, are shaped by our cultural setting, but not for the reasons that we are accustomed to think. The church chooses particular forms not to adapt to the customs, preferences, taste, or comfort level of the worshipers. Rather, her selection of song should be part of an effort to discern the ways in which she is tempted by worldliness, what it means to be set apart from the world, and how avoiding worldliness promotes holiness. To be sure, this is not the only standard for music, as if the church needs to choose something as different as possible from what her members have ever heard. But the church cannot forget her duty to avoid worldliness and so must be ever alert to the ways in which preferences for certain kinds of music may indeed reflect attitudes unbecoming of saints. If the church chooses music that imitates the prevailing standards of the world, she will do a poor job of equipping believers to be resistance fighters against worldliness, that is, to be a people set apart.

Contemporary Music

As we have already noted, advocates of praise and worship choruses encourage their use in worship because it is more intelligible to a younger generation of worshipers. But ironically, much of this music does not measure up even to this standard. The vague spirituality of these choruses often fails the test of intelligibility that Paul teaches in 1 Corinthians 14. It is far easier, for example, to understand what the Ebenezer is of "Come Thou Fount" than the river that flows in the chorus of "Shine, Jesus, Shine."

Furthermore, most of what falls under the label of contemporary worship music is not really up to date. John M. Frame concedes this in his book *Contemporary Worship Music* when he acknowledges that much of the music in popular praise songs resembles the "'soft rock' of the early 1970s."[5] Such "easy listening" music may reflect the preferences of aging baby boomers that have fond memories of adolescence, but it is a far cry from the rap and hip-hop music of the 1990s. This assessment has been seconded by even some of contemporary worship's most enthusiastic proponents. In his recent book *Reinventing American Protestantism,* Donald Miller notes how leaders of so-called "new paradigm churches" are wary of music that is truly contemporary: "In spite of the stress on cultural currency," he writes, "several people we interviewed noted the difficulty of incorporating some music styles, such as punk rock, into worship. Both Chuck Smith and John Wimber stated that the sensuality and violence that characterize music of the last decade are simply not congruent with Christian values."[6] This is, to say the least, a striking concession that makes the folks at Calvary Chapel sound remarkably traditionalist.

If the music of many praise songs comes from the style preferred by the me-generation, the language of these songs might also reflect a solipsistic orientation. For another characteristic feature of newer praise choruses is the predominance of the first-person personal pronoun. *I-me-my* is the prevailing perspective of the singer. Much of the older hymnody and psalmody displays a balance between individual and corporate expression of piety. In newer collections of praise songs, the overwhelming stress is on the individual, solitary ecstatic experience. Such themes are hardly conducive for worship that is supposed to embody the corporate solidarity of the people of God as they march to Zion.

Along with the movement away from communal piety, the focus of newer songs has shifted from God-centeredness to man-centeredness. Michael Horton has noted, for instance, that the emphasis in the psalms and older hymnody is on the work of God, specifically his faithfulness to his covenant. As he writes in *In the Face of God*, "the biblical text never gives us the subjective (my experience or my offering of praise or obedience) apart from the objective (God's saving work in Christ). . . . It never concentrates on what we are to do before establishing what God has already done."[7] By stressing the subjective experience, the new music eclipses the objective basis for our coming to worship. This is reinforced by the characteristic repetition in the lyrics that atrophies sustained theological reflection on God, on his attributes, and on his works. Singers of these songs may gain an experiential lift or spiritual high, but that high might come at the expense of being reminded that God's works are the Christian's only hope. By contrast the psalms engage in limited repetition, they are rich in content, and they stress the objective work of God in the salvation of his people, which is one more reason for leavening worship with regular singing of psalms.

Bringing Our Best

A Presbyterian theologian once prophesied about the damages attending the triumph of contemporary music in Presbyterian churches. "We shall in the end have a mass of corrupting religious poetry against which the church will have to wage a sore contest." That critic was Robert L. Dabney, and he wrote those words in 1876. Dabney spoke out against the popular gospel songs of the late Victorian era, especially the works of Dwight L. Moody's musician, Ira Sankey. As Dabney predicted, these songs found homes in most twentieth-century hymnals, eventually crowding out many hymns and psalms of earlier hymnals. The danger, Dabney warned, "is that of habituating the taste of Christians to a very vapid species of pious doggerel, containing the most diluted possible traces of saving truth, suitable to the most infantile faculties supplemented by a jingle of 'vain repetitions.' "[8] Dabney's remarks serve as a helpful reminder to us that the decline in the church's music is not entirely new. Changes in song did not happen only after 1960, nor did the advent of drums, guitars, and overhead projectors signal the end of a golden age. Likewise, the problem cannot be restricted to tunes with a Nashville copyright. American Protestantism has long been vulnerable to the trivializing influences of popular culture.

What criteria can we apply then in order to make sound judgments in our worship music? In a recent article in the *Westminster Theological Journal,* Terry L. Johnson offers four tests:

1. Is it singable? "The Reformation rightly restored *congregational* singing to the life of the church, replacing specialized choirs and vocalists," writes Johnson.[9] So we must ask of our music: can it be sung by untrained voices and can amateur musicians play it? Many churches have discovered how difficult new praise choruses are. Originating as performance music, these tunes are for the expert musicians and for trained soloists, duets, or choirs.

2. Is it biblically and theologically sound? Songs containing errors about God and his attributes, his works of creation, providence, and redemption have no place in worship that seeks to please him.

3. Is it biblically and theologically mature? The grandeur of Reformed theology must be reinforced by maturity in our song. Calvin wrote: "There must always be concern that the song be neither light nor frivolous but have gravity and majesty. ... There is a great difference between the music which one makes to entertain men at table and in their

homes and psalms which are sung in the church in the presence of God and his angels."[10]

4. Is it emotionally balanced? There is a difference between emotion and emotionalism, and a strong emotional appeal in our music without accompanying theological content is manipulative.

Hebrews reminds us that we need solid food to reach spiritual maturity. So Johnson writes: "it is crucial that the church's songs be substantial enough to express accurately mature Christian belief as well as the subtlety of Christian experience. . . . Simplistic, sentimental, repetitious songs by their very nature cannot carry the weight of Reformed doctrine and will leave the people of God ill-equipped on occasions of great moment."[11]

To alter the food metaphor slightly, pop music can be compared to fast-food. It is quick, easily consumed, and initially tasty. But it is usually not nutritious. Are we using forms of worship that provide nourishment to the soul? The experience of the people of God in the wilderness teaches us that good things do not happen to God's people when they abandon the manna that he has provided. Are our songs more like pop-tarts or broccoli?

Singing is popular in churches today. For this we should be grateful. But we should also be careful. How often do we look forward to an evening cantata from the choir because we will not have to sit through a sermon? Why do we think of these special music services as evangelistic opportunities to bring in the unchurched? These are common and wrong ways to think about worship music. They imply that we have forgotten that we are to "sing to the LORD a new song, for he has done marvelous things" (Ps. 98:1 RSV). In the end, the worship wars are not simply about new songs replacing old hymns, but reflect a reorientation of public worship away from the Word read and preached and toward the singing of songs. Worship music is threatening to undo the one trait that has always characterized Reformed worship, namely, the centrality of the Word. If this is the case, the worship wars are truly worth fighting. But this also means that the fight can't be waged over our preferences in music. It must be fought over the elements and nature of worship. Consequently, the contemporary debates about song in worship make all the more obvious our need for greater discernment.

Conclusion

Discernment
in Worship

Q How can we tell the difference between the true
church and the false church?

A The marks by which the true Church is known are the
pure preaching of the doctrine of the gospel; maintaining the pure administration of the sacraments as instituted by Christ; in short, if all things are managed according to the pure Word of God, all things contrary to it
rejected, and Jesus Christ acknowledged as the only head
of the Church. The false church will not submit to the
yoke of Christ; neither does she administer the sacraments as appointed by Christ in His Word, but adds to
and takes from them as she thinks proper; and she relies
more upon men than upon Christ. These two Churches
are easily known and distinguished from each other.

(Belgic Confession, art. 29)

Why have we written this book? We have tried to make a case for worship that is explicitly Reformed. But some readers may have found our reasoning archaic and perhaps even chauvinistic. After all, we live in postconfessional and even antidenominational times. Why ought we to strive any more for worship that is distinctively Reformed? Wasn't that style of worship simply a product of a particular age that no longer makes sense today? Others might wonder if the approach of this book is fundamentally narrow-minded and proud. Isn't it more humble and tolerant to be willing to blend into our worship the strengths of other denominational and confessional traditions? In other words, what's all the fuss? What's so bad about the newer forms of worship emerging recently in Presbyterian and Reformed churches?

As attractive as contemporary forms of worship might appear, the logic by which they have entered Reformed circles is destructive of the Reformed tradition because it makes theology powerless. It separates belief from practice. To be sure, many want to hold on to the tenets of Reformed theology, but often these advocates are not as concerned about Reformed practices such as worship. Consequently, we are still zealous for the Reformed confessions even as many proponents of the Reformed faith worship like Pentecostals. But is there any more pride entailed in practicing the Reformed faith than in professing it? It may be that those who affirm Reformed doctrines of salvation (i.e., the five points of Calvinism) but abandon Reformed worship are the ones guilty of narrow-mindedness. Our contention is that it is just as legitimate to argue for Reformed worship as it is to defend Reformed doctrine. And to call into question Reformed worship is to invite doubts about Reformed theology. Faith and practice cannot be separated; worship, therefore, flows from doctrine.

Another line of argument that downplays recent worship debates is one that points to church history and sees today's worship wars as merely contemporary versions of perennial struggles. The Reformation introduced new music, it is said, and so did the First and Second Great Awakenings. So also Presbyterians and Reformed debated in the nineteenth century, disputing the introduction of organs and choirs in public worship. Change is inevitable, and whenever there is change in the church controversy will inevitably follow. So if Reformed orthodoxy managed to survive changes in the past, why can't we expect it to incorporate today's worship innovations?

While this line of reasoning may reassure some, it misreads church history. The character of today's changes is different, and so that explanation, as comforting as it sounds, fails. The Reformation was not experimentation for its own sake, but was an effort to reform the church *according to the Word of God.* Can today's liturgical innovators claim that they are trying to eliminate unbiblical worship in favor of worship that conforms to God's Word? We think not because most of today's novelties in worship are offered as supplements rather than replacements to traditional Protestant worship. The analogy would be Luther and Calvin adding the congregational singing of hymns and Psalms on to the celebration of the Mass.

The reason for the worship wars today, then, is because the church has failed to exercise discernment over her worship. Conservative Presbyterians and Reformed have carefully preserved orthodoxy in their theology, but they have not been as diligent about worship. As we draw our study of Reformed worship to a close, some suggestions for the right way to evaluate worship would appear to be appropriate.

Wrong Ways to Evaluate

Let us first review how *not* to evaluate worship. One common mistake is to play the numbers game. This method says that the larger the church, the better its worship—or, at the very least, there must be something good going on in the worship of big churches. It is surprising how often Christians succumb to this logic. Followers of Jesus Christ should know better than to equate popularity with truth. As W. Robert Godfrey has pointed out, Jesus was the greatest church-planting failure in history, by the standards that the church-growth movement generally employs. In John, a great multitude gathered to meet Jesus by the Sea of Galilee, but he did not mistake the crowd for true disciples. He questioned their motives: ". . . you seek Me, not because you saw signs, but because you ate of the loaves and were filled" (6:26). Our Lord then went on to tell his audience that he is the bread of life, one better than the manna the Israelites ate in the wilderness because it gives eternal life (6:48–50). The response by the multitude was not the one predicted by many church planters. They said, "This is a difficult statement; who can listen to it?" (6:60) and then proceeded to abandon Jesus. By the end of his teaching, the number of disciples with Christ had dwindled to twelve.

The numbers game is one that Christians, especially Reformed Christians, will always lose. Consider these statistics: the circulation of *People* magazine is 3,600,000; *Christianity Today*'s is roughly 170,000, *The Outlook*'s about 4,500; and the *Westminster Theological Journal*'s 1,200. It is obvious which of these magazines is most popular. But which are the most edifying? The truths of the Reformed faith are indeed hard sayings to hear. Sinners do not naturally like to hear about their guilt and the consequences of their sin, nor their dependence on a suffering Savior for eternal life. Any conception of worship that suggests the Reformed faith can be easily packaged and so appeal to large numbers of men and women has not reckoned with the history of Reformed and Presbyterian churches.

This is not to suggest that smaller is always better. Of course we should yearn to see our churches filled, and we should remove unnecessary barriers to outsiders, that they are not offended by us and our ways. But we must also strive for a recovery of Reformed worship. The point is simply that size is not a reliable measure of faithfulness. In fact, large numbers should be read with a measure of suspicion since our Lord himself said, ". . . many are called, but few are chosen" (Matt. 22:14).

Another improper way to evaluate worship is by looking for sincerity or good motives. This is a sentimental standard that fails to recognize that people can be very sincerely committed to error. American slavery and Soviet communism each had its fervent disciples, but in neither case did devotion justify the cause. Consider, too, the recent growth of Islam and Mormonism. Their believers are sincere and have moving "experiences" in their worship. This does not make their beliefs true or their practices right.

So experience is no guide to true worship. What is just as important to notice is that a focus on experience deflects discernment from reliable indicators of acceptable worship. As J. Gresham Machen insisted, "truth [is] the foundation of conduct and doctrine the foundation of life."[1] To reverse this order and to make experience the foundation of theology is an error that repeats the mistake that was so characteristic of liberalism. And to look to experience for theology puts truth up for grabs. As Machen said of liberalism's stress on religious experience, "it denies not this truth or that but truth itself. It denies that there is any possibility of attaining to a truth that will always be true. There is truth, it holds, for this generation and truth for that generation, but no truth for all generations; there is truth for this race and truth for that race, but no truth for all races."[2] And so, if experience becomes the norm for worship, it is no wonder why so many services take forms that appeal to different generations and economic groups. True doctrine transcends these differences and may even unite diverse people in faithful worship. But experience will leave the young and old, suburban and rural, Asian and Anglo sequestered in worship services geared for each group's demographic niche.

Yet another example of impoverished discernment in worship is to let a profession of Christian faith become a basis for legitimacy. Just because someone claims to be a Christian, or even affirms Reformed theology, does not justify whatever he or she does in worship. Many today give the benefit of the doubt in worship to people who seem to be devout, as if Christian charity demands turning a blind eye to unwise or even sinful practices in such other areas as honoring parents or living a chaste life. To be sure, many who advocate the new kind of worship appear to be Bible-believing Christians. They appear to be devoted to Christ and are motivated by evangelistic concerns.

We should not, however, forget the lesson that the fundamentalist-modernist controversy painfully taught. Liberals claimed to be good Christians. They rejected the historic meaning of the church's creeds in order to get back to Christ and to the Bible. But conservatives like Machen thought liberals were not speaking truthfully. He argued that liberals, instead of accepting or rejecting the statements of the Apostles' Creed or the Westminster Confession of Faith, "merely 'interpret'" them. "Every generation, it is said, must interpret the Bible or the creed in its own way."[3] And so people who claimed to believe the same things as conservatives departed significantly from a basic understanding of the Christian religion. Of course, we are not claiming that worship innovators are inevitably liberal in the old-fashioned sense. But in Reformed circles, when it comes to the meaning of the Reformed creeds and catechisms in their teaching on worship, we do find a similar kind of evasiveness about the historic meaning of these confessional statements that govern Presbyterian and Reformed church life. The point is that people will sometimes employ biblical and confessional language, wrongly understood, to baptize worship innovations. The implication is that Christians should not merely take other believers at their word but also look at their deeds. And one of the telltale signs of whether a person, congregation, or denomination is Reformed is worship. For faith cannot be divorced from practice.

Together these flawed ways of evaluating worship call us back to the task of discernment. We must look beyond appearances and ask hard questions. Does theology come from our worship experience, or is the worship of our churches based on Reformed theology? Are we striving to be acceptable to God or to be relevant to visitors? Is our standard the Word of God or the wisdom of market research? Do people mean what they say when they claim their worship is reverent? Discernment in worship, in other words, requires that we look to the theology that undergirds our worship.

Reformed According to the Word

To avoid becoming liturgical relativists, then, will involve breaking with old and new ways of worship, and instead, seeking to worship at our best. Just as there are better and worse ways to express Christian theology, so there are better and worse ways of worshiping God. To be sure, there is no perfect worship until the new heavens and the new earth because there is no perfect church in this age. But humility must not provide license for relativism, and recognition of our sin and frailty should not detain us from striving to reform our worship as much as possible according to God's Word.

So what is the *best* that Presbyterian and Reformed congregations can offer? What is a better form of a sermon? One that conforms to the teaching of the Bible. What is a better form of prayer? One that asks for things that are agreeable to God's will as it is revealed in his Word. In other words, the best worship is that which conforms to the Bible. And for Presbyterians, it is not enough simply to use the words of the Bible, but also what the Bible teaches as a whole. This means that our theology, which is the system of doctrine taught in Scripture, will be an indispensable guide in determining what is best in worship. Reformed theology in its fullest expression, not the isolation of a few favorite doctrines, produces discernment because it systematically states the truth revealed in the Bible.

Of course, to say that the best worship is worship that is biblical is only another way of articulating the regulative principle of worship. Our only standard for worship is what is revealed in Scripture, not our emotions, or what church-growth experts recommend. God's Word is at the heart of Reformed worship, and it is the best way to be discerning about the way we gather to honor and give thanks to God.

This is precisely what the Belgic Confession teaches in article 29. It says that the way to spot a true church from a false one is by looking at worship. The true church will be "managed according to the pure Word of God, all things contrary to it rejected, and Jesus Christ acknowledged as the only head of the Church." This means that "the pure doctrine of the gospel" will be preached, "the pure administration of the sacraments" will be maintained, and church discipline will be exercised. (Discipline is evident in worship when the preaching is sound and sacraments are pure.) Interestingly, the marks of the true church have little to do with the kind of songs sung, whether a congregation is seeker-sensitive, or what kind of Sunday school curriculum a church offers. For this reason, some might find that the Belgic Confession has little to say about discernment in worship. But the point of this book is that it has boatloads to say about our priorities in worship. If Reformed and Presbyterian believers were content with preaching, the sacraments, and church discipline, the worship wars would not be happening. As it is, we have lost sight of the calling of the church and the centrality of worship to that calling. But the Belgic Confession is right. The church acknowledges Christ as her head when her marks are evident. And if those marks are not obvious, then the church is false, "ascribes more power and authority to herself and her ordinances than to the Word of God, . . . will not submit herself to the yoke of Christ," and relies "more upon men than on Christ."

Discernment lies not in reclaiming the tradition or rejecting the novel but in rediscovering the nature and purpose of the church and the centrality of worship in the lives of God's saints. As the Belgic Confession indicates, discerning true worship is not difficult. But our age has made worship mysterious by trying to make it do more than it was intended to do. So to restore Reformed worship to its rightful and recognizable place, we return with the Bible and confessions as our guides to some liturgical basics:

Reformed worship is founded on the Word of God. The Word not only directs our worship, as we have seen, but it also comprises our worship. It is read, it is sung, and it is preached. Moreover, the Word is seen, felt, and tasted, in the Lord's Supper and baptism.

Reformed worship is theocentric. Worship is God-centered because its aim is the glory of God. It is the highest form of fellowship between God and his people, and it must be done in Spirit and truth. The Bible reveals that there is nothing that God hates more than false worship. John Murray described Reformed piety as God-consciousness, "an all-pervasive sense of God's presence." This spirituality should characterize all of life, but especially the gathering of the saints for public worship. "Adoration springs from the apprehension of God's majesty," Murray continues, "and where this is, there must be reverence, that is, godly fear. Here again much of our worship falls under the charge of irreverence and therefore under condemnation. There is a place in life for jollity and jollification. But how alien to the worship of God would this be in the sanctuary."[4] (It may be interesting to remember that Murray did not live to see the phenomenon of "Praise & Worship" or blended worship.)

Reformed worship nurtures God's people through the means of grace. God has constituted us in such a way that worship strengthens our spiritual lives. He knows that we are weak, he knows our frame, and worship is his sustenance for our warfare with sin and temptation. Worship is not an extra part of the Christian life. It is the minimum spiritual diet for a life of faith and repentance.

Reformed worship is dialogical. Worship is a meeting between God and his people. Believers come at his invitation, are welcomed into his presence. God speaks through the invocation, the reading of the Word, sermon, sacraments, and the benediction. Worshipers respond in song, prayer, and confession of faith. The service is a holy conversation between heaven and earth. It cannot be repackaged as a form of entertainment or congregational meeting.

Reformed worship is simple. As recipients of the fuller revelation of Christ, we worship as the church come of age, not the church underage. We are not dependent on the fleshly and childish elements of the Old Covenant. The Reformed tradition expresses simplicity in worship by making the Bible central throughout all parts of the service. Simplicity in worship is also evident in a stable routine—an order of service that is set, that is habitual, that lacks spectacle. Observance of the Sabbath is another way of demonstrating simplicity in worship. Reformed believers do not need to observe other holy days in order to show their devotion and receive God's blessing. Instead, by routinely observing one entire day out of every seven, believers are treated to the feast of God's merciful provision in the outward and ordinary means of grace.

Reformed worship is eschatological. We are resurrected with Christ, and we worship him in heaven. Our union with the resurrected and ascended Lord challenges the mistaken idea that we need visible or material supports in worship. As reverent and as worshipful as an ornate Gothic cathedral may seem, it is actually carnal, in the sense that it keeps us earthbound, when in worship we should be heavenbound. Worship is a foretaste of glory, not a barrier to longing for Christ's return.

The Best Worship "Style"

Frequently, variety in worship is described as the difference in style, whether contemporary or traditional, seeker-sensitive or liturgical. These styles do not affect content, supposedly, but are interchangeable according to the needs and preferences of the congregation. But from a biblical perspective this is the wrong way to think about worship style. In Scripture there are ultimately only two styles of worship: true and false.

In his book *The Southern Tradition*, historian Eugene Genovese contrasts religious practices on the competing sides of the Mason-Dixon line in this way:

> In the North people are wont to say, "You worship God in your way, and we'll worship Him in *ours*." This delightful formulation says, in effect, that since religion is of little consequence anyway, why argue? In contrast, the Southern version . . . says: "You worship God in your way, and we'll worship Him in *His*."[5]

However accurately this may characterize regional differences in American Christianity, this is a helpful way of distinguishing competing claims of good worship. Are we pleasing man or God? Are we striving for God's glory or for human comfort and enjoyment? Are we satisfying seekers or honoring the one who seeks his worshipers (John 4:23)?

The Belgic Confession defines the true church as one where Christ is Lord, and where he is truly its head (art. 31). It is a church governed by the Word as the only reliable way to know the will of Christ. This should be true of our worship. True worship is worship where Christ is truly acknowledged as Lord and where it conforms to what Christ has taught in his Word by himself and his apostles. We can distinguish true worship from false worship by what God has revealed through his Holy Spirit.

Conservative Presbyterians have been generally discerning about doctrinal fidelity. They can defend sound theology and identify the defects of Trinitarian, christological, or soteriological heresies. But are they as astute about maintaining the ways in which correct doctrine takes visible form in the lives and practices of the organized church? Reformed orthodoxy will die a slow and certain death if it has nothing to say about the way we order our lives.

And that death will be especially painful if it is silent about our highest calling. Worship, we have noted, is the most fundamental aspect of the Christian life. To worship God is to engage in the highest calling of our creation as God's servants and image bearers. To worship acceptably, we must worship with discernment. And we must have courage. For it is not enough to spot false worship. We must be able to call it that when we see it.

In the end, Reformed theology is only as good, only as compelling, and only as binding, as Reformed worship. And that is what the fuss is all about.

Notes

Introduction: Sound Doctrine and Worship

1. John Calvin, *Institutes of the Christian Religion*, ed. John T. McNeill, trans. Ford Lewis Battles, 2 vols. (Philadelphia: Westminster, 1960), 1.11.8 (1:108).

Chapter 1: The Church and the World

1. J. Gresham Machen, *God Transcendent*, ed. Ned Bernard Stonehouse (Edinburgh: Banner of Truth, 1982), p. 104.

2. David F. Wells, *God in the Wasteland: The Reality of Truth in a World of Fading Dreams* (Grand Rapids: Eerdmans, 1994), p. 39.

3. Ibid.

4. Machen, *God Transcendent*, p. 108.

5. R. B. Kuiper, *The Glorious Body of Christ* (Grand Rapids: Eerdmans, 1958), pp. 59, 60.

6. J. Gresham Machen, *What Is Christianity?* (Grand Rapids: Eerdmans, 1951), p. 238.

7. Kuiper, *Glorious Body*, p. 253.

8. Machen, *God Transcendent*, p. 108.

Chapter 2: The Purpose of the Church

1. Rick Warren, *The Purpose Driven Church: Growth without Compromising Your Message and Mission* (Grand Rapids: Zondervan, 1995).

2. David Neff, ed., "100 Things the Church Is Doing Right," *Christianity Today* 41 (Nov. 17, 1997): 13–42.

3. Albert Barnes, *The Church and Slavery* (New York: Negro Universities Press, 1969), pp. 21–22.

4. James Henley Thornwell, *The Collected Writings of James Henley Thornwell*, 4 vols. (Edinburgh: Banner of Truth Trust, 1974), 4: 382–83.

5. George Barna, *Marketing the Church* (Colorado Springs: NavPress, 1990), p. 17.

6. This is the mission statement of Campus Crusade for Christ.

7. Edmund P. Clowney, *The Church* (Downers Grove, Ill.: InterVarsity, 1995), p. 160.

8. John Calvin, *Commentary on a Harmony of the Evangelists: Matthew, Mark, and Luke,* 3 vols. (Grand Rapids: Baker, 1979), 3:391 (Calvin's comment is on Matt. 28:20).

9. C. John Miller, *Outgrowing the Ingrown Church* (Grand Rapids: Zondervan, 1986), p. 57.

10. Thornwell, *Collected Writings,* 4:383–84.

11. John Calvin, *Institutes of the Christian Religion,* ed. John T. McNeill, trans. Ford Lewis Battles, 2 vols. (Philadelphia: Westminster, 1960), 4.8.8 (2:1155).

Chapter 3: A Worshiping Community

1. William Willimon, *Peculiar Speech: Preaching to the Baptized* (Grand Rapids: Eerdmans, 1992), p. 114.

2. Peter J. Leithart, "Cult and Culture," *First Things* 29 (Jan. 1993): 7.

3. From a bulletin of the Community Church of Joy in Phoenix, Arizona.

Chapter 4: The Holy Day of Worship

1. John M. Frame, *Worship in Spirit and Truth* (Phillipsburg, N.J.: P&R, 1996), p. 42.

2. Ibid., p. 34.

3. Ibid., pp. 42–43. Emphasis added.

Chapter 5: Acceptable Worship

1. John Calvin, *Institutes of the Christian Religion,* ed. John T. McNeill, trans. Ford Lewis Battles, 2 vols. (Philadelphia: Westminster, 1960), 4.10.11 (2:1190).

2. John Calvin, *The Necessity of Reforming the Church* (Audubon, N.J.: Old Paths, 1994), p. 7.

3. Quoted in Carlos M. N. Eire, *War against the Idols: The Reformation of Worship from Erasmus to Calvin* (Cambridge: Cambridge University, 1986), p. 208.

4. T. David Gordon, "The Regulative Principle of Worship: The Argument from Charity," *Nicotine Theological Journal* 1:4 (Oct. 1997): 1–3.

5. Hughes Oliphant Old, *Worship That Is Reformed According to Scripture* (Atlanta: John Knox, 1984), p. 177.

Chapter 6: Reformed Liturgy

1. John M. Frame, *Worship in Spirit and Truth* (Phillipsburg, N.J.: P&R, 1996), p. 1.

2. Robert G. Rayburn, *O Come, Let Us Worship: Corporate Worship in the Evangelical Church* (Grand Rapids: Baker, 1980), pp. 20–21.

3. T. David Gordon, from an unpublished paper.

4. Orthodox Presbyterian Church, *Directory for Worship*, 2.2 (in *Book of Church Order of the Orthodox Presbyterian Church* [Philadelphia: Committee on Christian Education of the OPC, 2000], p. 135).

5. "Liturgical Committee Report," *Acts of Synod of the Christian Reformed Church* (Grand Rapids: Christian Reformed, 1968), pp. 135–36.

6. Orthodox Presbyterian Church, *Directory for Worship*, 2.2.

7. Orthodox Presbyterian Church, *Directory for Worship*, 3.1.

8. Terry L. Johnson, *Leading in Worship* (Oak Ridge, Tenn.: Covenant Foundation, 1996), p. 15.

9. Terry L. Johnson, "The Pastor's Public Ministry: Part 1," *Westminster Theological Journal* 60 (1980): 140.

Chapter 7: Leading and Participating in Worship

1. John M. Timmerman, "Whatever Happened to Sunday?" *Reformed Journal* (Feb. 1981), p. 14.

2. Rick Warren, *The Purpose Driven Church: Growth without Compromising Your Message and Mission* (Grand Rapids: Zondervan, 1995), pp. 368, 375–78.

3. A very helpful article on this subject is T. David Gordon, " 'Equipping' Ministry in Ephesians 4," *Journal of the Evangelical Theological Society* 37 (1994): 69–78.

Chapter 8: Worship with Godly Fear

1. John Calvin, *Institutes of the Christian Religion*, ed. John T. McNeill, trans. Ford Lewis Battles, 2 vols. (Philadelphia: Westminster, 1960), 1.2.2 (1:43).

2. Edward Farley, "A Missing Presence," *Christian Century* 115 (March 18–25, 1998): 276.

3. Walt Kallestad, *Entertainment Evangelism: Taking the Church Public* (Nashville: Abingdon, 1996), p. 68.

4. John M. Frame, *Worship in Spirit and Truth* (Phillipsburg, N.J.: P&R, 1996), p. 84.

5. Calvin, *Institutes*, 1.2.2 (1:43).

Chapter 9: The Means of Grace

1. Edmund P. Clowney, *The Church* (Downers Grove, Ill.: InterVarsity, 1995), p. 89.

2. John Calvin, *Commentaries on the Epistle of Paul to the Galatians and Ephesians* (Grand Rapids: Baker, 1979), p. 141. (Calvin's remarks are on Gal. 4:26).

3. John Calvin, *Institutes of the Christian Religion*, ed. John T. McNeill, trans. Ford Lewis Battles, 2 vols. (Philadelphia: Westminster, 1960), 4.14.5 (2:1280).

4. Ibid., 4.14.19 (2:1284).

Chapter 10: Elements, Circumstances, and Forms

1. Evelyn Underhill, *Worship* (London: Nisbet, 1937), p. 287.

2. John Calvin, The *Necessity of Reforming the Church* (Audubon, N.J.: Old Paths, 1994), p. 6.

3. T. David Gordon, unpublished paper.

4. John Calvin, *Institutes of the Christian Religion*, ed. John T. McNeill, trans. Ford Lewis Battles, 2 vols. (Philadelphia: Westminster, 1960), 4.17.44 (2:1422).

5. Orthodox Presbyterian Church, *Directory for the Public Worship of God*, 2:7.

6. Ibid., 3:2.

7. Ibid., 3:3.

8. Charles Hodge, "Presbyterian Liturgies," *Biblical Repertory and Princeton Review* 27 (1855): 461.

9. Terry L. Johnson, *Leading in Worship* (Oak Ridge, Tenn.: Covenant Foundation), p. 5.

Chapter 11: Song in Worship

1. Martin Luther, *What Luther Says: An Anthology*, ed. Ewald M. Plass (St. Louis: Concordia, 1959), p. 982.

2. John Calvin, *Epistle to the Reader* (quoted in: Charles Garside, Jr. *The Origin of Calvin's Theology of Music, 1536–1543.* (Philadelphia: American Philosophical Society, 1979, p. 33).

3. Hughes Oliphant Old, *Worship That Is Reformed According to Scripture* (Atlanta: John Knox, 1984), p.55.

4. Diana West, "Against Conservative Cool," *Weekly Standard* 1:45 (Aug. 5, 1996): 22.

5. John M. Frame, *Contemporary Worship Music: A Biblical Defense* (Phillipsburg, N.J.: P&R, 1997), p. 7.

6. Donald E. Miller, *Reinventing American Protestantism: Christianity in the New Millennium* (Berkeley: University of California, 1997), p. 84.

7. Michael Horton, *In the Face of God* (Dallas: Word, 1996), p. 214.

8. Robert Lewis Dabney, "Lay Preaching," in *Discussions: Evangelical and Theological*, 3 vols. (Edinburgh: Banner of Truth Trust, 1967), 2: 94–95.

9. Terry L. Johnson, "The Pastor's Public Ministry, Part 1," *Westminster Theological Journal* 60 (Spring 1998): 148.

10. John Calvin, quoted in Garside, p. 32.

11. Johnson, "The Pastor's Public Ministry," p. 149.

Conclusion: Discernment in Worship

1. J. Gresham Machen, *Christian Faith in the Modern World* (New York: Macmillan, 1936), p. 88.

2. Ibid., p. 90.

3. J. Gresham Machen, *God Transcendent* (Grand Rapids: Eerdmans, 1949), p. 47.

4. John Murray, "Worship," in *Collected Writings of John Murray*, 4 vols. (Edinburgh: Banner of Truth Trust, 1976), 1:167.

5. Eugene D. Genovese, *The Southern Tradition: The Achievement and Limitations of an American Conservatism* (Cambridge: Harvard University, 1994), p. 25.

General Index

adoption, 140
already/not yet, 56
Anabaptists, 59
Anglicans, 78, 93, 154
antithesis, 32–33
Apostles' Creed, 30, 181
assimilation, 46
assurance, 97, 99, 140–41, 143
attitude, for worship, 19

baby boomers, 170
baptism, 43, 47, 73, 114–15, 142
Barna, George, 42
Barnes, Albert, 40, 41, 42
benediction, 97, 100
benefits of redemption, 140–42
Bennett, William, 168
Bible:
  centrality, 93, 174
  as standard for worship, 77–85, 87, 182–83
blasphemy, 48, 127
blended worship, 20–21

blessing, 96–97, 98, 100, 102, 133–34, 143
boredom, 17, 115, 120, 138
Bourgeois, Louis, 165

calling, 68, 106
Calvary Chapel, 170
Calvin, John, 15, 44, 46, 58, 69, 79, 80, 82, 83–84, 100, 112, 119, 121, 138–39, 142, 148, 149–50, 161, 165, 166, 172, 178
Calvinists, 14, 83
casual worship, 125, 126
catechism memorizing, 155
celebration, 17–18, 128
ceremonial law, 81
ceremonies, 121
charismatic movement, 93, 154
choirs, 148, 166, 172, 178
Christian liberty, 81, 84–85, 152

Christian life, as pilgrimage, 55–58, 136–37, 141
Christian nurture, 46
Christian Reformed Church, 92, 107, 109
Christianity Today, 39
church:
  as agent of social reform, 40–41
  antithetical to world, 25–26, 32–33, 39, 60, 164
  as business, 42
  as countercultural, 141
  as gathered community, 19
  marks, 47, 53–54, 111, 183
  as mother, 138–39
  as pilgrim people, 55
  purpose, 39–42
church activities, 58, 64
church architecture, 148
church growth movement, 41–42
church history, 178

195

Index of Scripture

Index of Confessions
and Catechisms

D. G. Hart(Ph.D., Johns Hopkins University) is director for honors programs and faculty development at the Intercollegiate Studies Institute in Wilmington, Delaware. The author and editor of fourteen volumes, Hart has been director of the Institute for the Study of American Evangelicals, librarian and professor of church history at Westminster Theological Seminary, and academic dean and professor of church history at Westminster Seminary in California. He has also served as book-review editor of *Fides et Historia*, editor of the *Westminster Theological Journal*, and book-review editor of *Modern Reformation*.

John R. Muether(M.A.R., Westminster Theological Seminary) is librarian and associate professor of church history at Reformed Theological Seminary in Orlando. The coauthor of three volumes, Muether has served on the Harvard Divinity School library staff and has been librarian at Western Theological Seminary and at Westminster Theological Seminary. He has served on the editorial board of *Regeneration Quarterly* and on the board of directors of Mars Hill Audio. He is historian of the Orthodox Presbyterian Church and serves on that denomination's Christian Education Committee.

Hart and Muether are coauthors of *Fighting the Good Fight: A Brief History of the Orthodox Presbyterian Church.*